THE HISTORY AND DEVELOPMENT
OF THE FOURTH AMENDMENT
TO THE UNITED STATES
CONSTITUTION

Da Capo Press Reprints in

AMERICAN CONSTITUTIONAL AND LEGAL HISTORY

GENERAL EDITOR: LEONARD W. LEVY
Brandeis University

THE HISTORY AND DEVELOPMENT OF THE FOURTH AMENDMENT TO THE UNITED STATES CONSTITUTION

BY NELSON B. LASSON

DA CAPO PRESS • NEW YORK • 1970

A Da Capo Press Reprint Edition

This Da Capo Press edition of *The History and Development of the Fourth Amendment to the United States Constitution* is an unabridged republication of the first edition published originally in Baltimore in 1937 as Series LV, Number 2, in *The Johns Hopkins University Studies in Historical and Political Science.*

Library of Congress Catalog Card Number 75-87389
SBN 306-71532-5

THE HISTORY AND DEVELOPMENT OF THE
FOURTH AMENDMENT TO THE UNITED
STATES CONSTITUTION

THE HISTORY AND DEVELOPMENT OF THE FOURTH AMENDMENT TO THE UNITED STATES CONSTITUTION

By

NELSON B. LASSON, Ph. D., LL. B.

Lecturer in Political Science
University of Maryland

BALTIMORE

THE JOHNS HOPKINS PRESS

1937

PRINTED IN THE UNITED STATES OF AMERICA
BY J. H. FURST COMPANY, BALTIMORE, MARYLAND

TO MY FATHER

" The right of the people to be secure in their persons, houses, papers, and effects, against unreasonable searches and seizures, shall not be violated, and no Warrants shall issue, but upon probable cause, supported by oath or affirmation, and particularly describing the place to be searched, and the persons or things to be seized."

Article IV, Amendments to the Constitution of the United States.

PREFACE

The writer has attempted in the succeeding pages to present the constitutional history and law of the Fourth Amendment, a safeguard to the liberty of the individual which has come into especial prominence within the last several decades. It has been his endeavor to examine carefully the history of the Amendment and to survey analytically the cases decided by the final authority on the interpretation of the guaranty, the Supreme Court of the United States.

The writer wishes to acknowledge his grateful indebtedness to Professors W. W. Willoughby and James Hart, under whom he worked at The Johns Hopkins University, for their interested and kindly assistance in the preparation of this study. He is also indebted to Dr. Johannes Mattern and Dr. Richard M. Haywood, of the same university, for their help on part of the first chapter.

NELSON B. LASSON.

Washington, D. C.

CONTENTS

PAGE

Chapter   I. Early Background 13

Chapter II. Writs of Assistance in the Colonies...... 51

Chapter III. The Fourth Amendment............... 79

Chapter IV. Development of the Principle by the Su-
            preme Court 106

Table of Cases................................... 145

Table of Statutes................................ 149

Index 151

THE HISTORY AND DEVELOPMENT OF THE FOURTH AMENDMENT TO THE UNITED STATES CONSTITUTION

CHAPTER I

EARLY BACKGROUND

The antecedent history of the Fourth Amendment to the Constitution concerns itself primarily with those events which took place in England, in France, and in the American Colonies, in the thirty years preceding the adoption of the Amendment, which were immediately and directly the moving factors in the elevating of the principle of reasonable search and seizure to a constitutional instead of a merely legal significance. Prior to this period, however, there are several hundred years of English history in which also appear many instances of arbitrary and unrestricted and, for the most part, unchallenged powers in this regard.

Before entering into a discussion of this historical background, it may be of interest to look back for a moment upon several aspects of the subject even more remóte. The peculiar immunity that the law has thrown around the dwelling house of man, pithily expressed in the maxim, " a man's house is his castle," was not an invention of English jurisprudence. Even in ancient times there were evidences of that same concept in custom and law, partly as a result of the natural desire for privacy, partly an outgrowth, in all probability, of the emphasis placed by the ancients upon the home as a place of hospitality, shelter, and protection.

Biblical literature affords a number of illustrative instances of a relatively strong respect for the dwelling as a place which was not subject to arbitrary visitation, even on the part of official authority. In the story concerning Achan, Joshua did not send his messengers to search for and seize the prohibited articles in Achan's tent, even after his detection, until the latter had first confessed both his deed and the place where the articles were concealed.[1] Indeed, it seems that under the Hebrew law there was little or no occasion for the question to arise, since the cases appear to turn solely upon the testimony of witnesses. The extreme solicitude in such matters shown by the authorities of that particular jurisprudence is demonstrated in a passage of the Talmud which states that no writ of replevin of personal property is to be granted by the court when the bailee of that property *denies its possession* before the court, for to do so would make it appear that the court issued a writ, the execution of which was not certain. The rule goes on to hold that where the bailee *admits possession,* but not ownership by the plaintiff, a writ might be issued.[2]

Where the point does arise incidentally in certain civil cases, a right not to be disturbed in the occupation of the home seems everywhere to be upheld. One old leading commentator broadly states as a principle of ancient law that no one could enter the house of another without express permission.[3] By Biblical law a creditor is forbidden to enter his debtor's house to get security for his debt but must wait outside for the bringing forth of the pledge.[4] Even a bailiff of the court is enjoined from entering for that purpose.[5] And the high regard that the law had for the home is reflected in the protection with which it sought to surround it by punishing housebreaking at night with the death penalty.[6]

---

[1] Joshua 7: 10-26. Earlier in the same book we find that when the king of Jericho received information of the presence of the spies in the dwelling of Rachab, he did not thereupon dispatch a searching party to that place, but sent a message ordering Rachab to produce them. This gave her the opportunity to conceal the spies and throw their pursuers off the track. *Ibid.* 2: 1-7. Note also the apparent hesitation of the crowd, even in a community of the enlightenment of Sodom, in front of the house of Lot and the demand, before any attempt was made to force an entry, that he bring out the strangers he had sheltered. Genesis 19: 4-11.

[2] Michael L. Rodkinson, *The Babylonian Talmud* (Boston, 1918), V, 158.

[3] Rosh, in the *Hosen Mishpat*, chap. 389, sec. 5.

[4] Deuteronomy 24: 10.   [5] Rodkinson, VI, 113.

[6] W. W. Davies, *Codes of Hammurabi and Moses* (Cincinnati, 1915), p. 33. Article 21 of the Code of Hammurabi, a contemporary of Abraham, provides: " If a man makes a breach into a house, one

In Roman history and law there are also instances of the prevalence of similar ideas. According to the primitive view, the house was not only an asylum but was under the special protection of the household gods, who dwelt and were worshipped there.[7] If even an enemy reached the fireplace of the house, we read that he was sure of protection.[8] Cicero expressed the general feeling in this matter when he said in one of his orations: "What is more inviolable, what better defended by religion than the house of a citizen. . . . This place of refuge is so sacred to all men, that to be dragged from thence is unlawful."[9]

As regards Roman criminal procedure, the prosecution in most cases was a private one and began with the accusation of one party by another, before the proper court, of the commission of some criminal offense. A number of safeguards against oppression were thrown around the accused which are of particular interest here. The accuser had to state the grounds of his action and take oath that his suit was not vexatious or frivolous. If the suit proved in the end to be such, the defendant had an action for malicious prosecution, an offense punishable at that time by fine or imprisonment. The court in addition had to be satisfied that there was sub-

---

shall kill him in front of the breach, and bury him in it." Cf. Exodus 22: 2, 3. The code may also be found in A. Kocourek and J. H. Wigmore, *Sources of Ancient and Primitive Law* (Boston, 1915), pp. 395 ff.

[7] J. B. Moyle, *Imperatoris Iustiniani Institutionem* (Oxford, 1923), p. 515.

[8] Example of Coriolanus and Aufidius, cited by the South Carolina patriot of the Revolutionary War, Judge William Henry Drayton, in his charge to the grand jury in 1776. Hezekiah Niles, *Principles and Acts of the Revolution* (Baltimore, 1822), p. 88.

[9] Professor Radin states that many of the safeguards against oppression found in our present-day bills of rights were maintained in Roman law as general principles and embodied in maxims which were frequently cited. "The famous maxim 'every man's house is his castle' cited by Coke, 5 Rep. 92, and generally regarded as a peculiarly English privilege, comes directly from the Roman law. *Nemo de domo sua extrahi debet.*" But as has been indicated above, it would seem that the concept far antedates that body of law.

Professor Radin goes on to say that the criminal systems of England and all other modern states, until the 19th century, were far more rigid and less humane than the Roman system adopted by the Corpus Juris. Max Radin, *Roman Law* (St. Paul, 1927), pp. 475-476.

stantial and probable cause for the complaint. The suit
was then held over and a certain period of time set for an
investigation by the accuser.[10]

These salutary precautions having been observed, however,
the accuser was allowed quite a bit of latitude in his investigation. This was a function which was left entirely to him
to carry out. He was granted two kinds of precepts or warrants. One was an official writ of the court, which stated the
names of the parties and the nature of the accusation and
commanded all officials or other individuals to assist the complainant in the gathering of evidence and the summoning of
witnesses. The other was a statement of the law that regulated the procedure of gathering the evidence. It provided
that all papers and documents relating to the case were at
the disposal of the prosecutor [11] and everyone was placed
under pain of penalty for resistance to the proper execution
of the precept.[12] Armed with these warrants, the accuser
had what apparently amounted to a general power of search
for the desired documentary evidence. He could search the
house of the defendant or of any other person.[13] Cicero tells
of a number of these formal searches in his prosecution of
Verres.[14] The wording of the law set forth in the writ

[10] A. W. Zumpt, *Criminalprocess der römischen Republik* (Leipzig,
1871), pp. 142 ff., 150 ff.

[11] *Ibid.*, pp. 304 ff.

[12] *Ibid.*, p. 195.

[13] *Ibid.*, pp. 307-308, and note, p. 308; A. H. J. Greenidge, *Legal
Procedure of Cicero's Time* (New York, 1901), pp. 493-494.

[14] Cicero, *The Verrine Orations* (tr. L. H. G. Greenwood, New York,
1928), I, Bk. i, pp. 19, 50; Bk. ii, pp. 74, 182; II, Bk. iii, pp. 66, 154.
In certain cases, such as those concerning election frauds, the accused
had a competence probably equal to that of the accuser regarding
search for documentary evidence. See Zumpt, p. 305 n.; Theodor
Mommsen, *Römisches Strafrecht* (Leipzig, 1899), p. 420.

According to authorities, this right of search for evidence seems
to have been a principle dating from very early times. See Gustav
Geib, *Geschichte des römischen Criminalprocesses* (Leipzig, 1842),
p. 144. His citation, however, of an incident in Diony., IV, 48, 57,
is a doubtful precedent, since there the accused practically requested
the search to be made. See also Mommsen, p. 418.

In case of abuse of power, the complaint could be made to the
praetor in Rome or to the consul in the provinces, but the warrant
was so general that these officials, according to Zumpt (p. 308),
could give little protection.

Cicero had was so general that his authority to search everywhere seems to have been practically unlimited.

When it came, however, to the seizing and the taking away of documents and records, the Roman law showed itself a little more thoughtful of the interests of the accused and took precautions to prevent any forging or insertion of evidential papers.[15] The accuser had to seal up the documents in the presence of witnesses and within a certain time deliver what he had taken to the court. The court then, as its first duty in the case, had to examine the seal and investigate the attestation of the witnesses.[16]

The search for stolen goods was another field in which the question of search and seizure was involved. In this situation the law displayed a greater concern for safeguarding the suspected person. Here we find a peculiar combination of modern legal principle and primitive ceremonialism. The victim of a theft, before he could institute a search in the house of a suspect, *had to describe with particularity* the goods he was seeking. This precaution, it will be remembered, was lacking in the method of gathering evidence discussed above.[17] The next step was the procedure called *lance et licio,*—as old, incidentally, as the Twelve Tables. This

---

[15] See the citations to Cicero's *Verrine Orations* in Greenidge, p. 494.

[16] The weight given documentary evidence in the time of the juristic classics was such that, according to Geib, once the authenticity of a document was proven, all contradictory testimony of witnesses was simply excluded, a rule that was also recognized in later periods. But as the weight accorded this form of evidence increased, a limitation appeared which Geib finds it difficult to reconcile with the spirit of inquisitorial procedure. This limitation was that the production of documents could not be compelled. This exemption stands in such remarkable contradiction to that procedure that Geib hardly considers it an all-embracing principle of the period. He prefers to suppose that since in certain crimes search was permitted, the rule had some exceptions. Geib, pp. 644 ff.

[17] Mommsen, p. 748, quoting the following passage in Paulus, 2, 31, 22: *Qui furtum quaesiturus est, antequam quaerat, debet dicere, quid quaerat et rem suo nomine et sua specie designare.* Mommsen also cites a provision in the *Digest* (11, 4, 1, 8a) which required particularity in the description of fugitive slaves for whom search was to be made. See C. H. Monro's translation of the *Digest of Justinian* (Cambridge, 1909), II, 237 ff.; A. F. von Pauly, *Real-Encyclopädie der classischen Altertumswissenschaft* (Stuttgart, 1912), VII, 393-394.

was a ceremony which, although outwardly a mere form, reveals an underlying practical purpose. Clad only in an apron (*licio*), and bearing a platter in his hand (*lance*), the person whose goods had been stolen entered and searched, in the presence of witnesses, the house where the goods were suspected to be.[18] He was ordinarily accompanied in his search by a bailiff of the court, who represented his legal authority; by a public crier, who proclaimed the theft of the various articles; and by a community slave, who broke open doors whenever necessary. If anyone offered resistance to the search or refused to give up the property if and when it was discovered, he was punished with the same penalty as attached to the theft itself.[19]

As regards Anglo-Saxon England, the Roman laws and institutions implanted in that country during the régime of the Empire exercised, in general, a strong influence upon later Anglo-Saxon law.[20] However, due to the scantiness of material concerning what was, at the most, an undeveloped legal system of a primitive civilization, the information which is available concerning this period is not particularly helpful. The fact, that the system of frankpledge and proof by compurgation and ordeal which existed then seems to have done away to a great extent with the necessity of discovering specific evidence of wrongdoing, no doubt also has much to do with this situation. Broadly speaking, however, there were indications of a regard for the privilege of the individual not to be disturbed in the peaceful occupancy of his home. The law, for example, recognized the crime of *hamsocn* (or *ham-*

---

[18] The apron as the sole article of apparel was prescribed evidently to prevent concealing of objects in the garments and " planting " them in someone's house in order to place a false charge. The platter, Mommsen says, was probably a symbol of the intended seizure and carrying away of the goods. According to Petronius, however, the searcher carried in the platter the stipulated reward, together with a certain " caution-money " by which he pledged himself to secrecy to his informer. See Mommsen, pp. 748-749, and notes.

[19] *Ibid.*, citing *Institutes*, 4, 1, 4. Later on, in the time of Justinian and Plautus, these searches were undertaken and conducted by public officers and not by the complainant. Moyle, p. 516 n.

[20] See the introduction to John Reeves' *History of English Law* (Finlason ed., Philadelphia, 1880), I, lxii ff.

fare), an offense the whole gist of which was solely the forcible entry into a man's dwelling, a " *domus invasio.*" [21] Throughout the laws of Anglo-Saxon and Norman times this offense was looked upon with great severity, justifying the killing of the perpetrator in the act without the payment of compensation usual in those days.[22] In the reign of King Edmund (940-946) the law provided that the person who committed this crime should forfeit all of his property, and even his life if the king so willed.[23]

Alfred the Great (871-891) was a king who seemed to be most solicitous of the rights of his subjects. One old work gives several examples which are of particular interest here and indicate how, at least during Alfred's reign, judges who valued their heads had to be careful not to make mistakes. The *Mirrour of Justices* relates,[24] among other such instances, that Alfred " hanged Ostline because he judged Seaman to death by a false warrant, grounded upon false suggestion, which supposed Seaman to be a person in the warrant, which he was not." And " he hanged Maclin, because he hanged Helgrave by warrant of indictment not special." [25]

Magna Carta frequently has been cited as one of the foun-

---

[21] See the definitions of *hamsocn* in *Ancient Laws and Institutes of England* (London, 1840), II, Glossary; *Select Pleas of the Crown* (W. Maitland, ed.), " Selden Society Publications " (London, 1888), I, 142; Henry de Bracton, *Legibus et Consuetudinibus Angliae* (as translated in No. 70 of the Chronicles of Great Britain and Ireland, London, 1883), II, 464, 465. The force of the distinction between this offense and those that were aggravations thereof is well brought out in a case that came up in the year 1201: " Roger appeals William for that he came with armed hand and with his force, and broke his houses *in hamsoken*, and *in felony* robbed him of six marks of silver," etc. *Select Pleas*, p. 43. See also cases 60, 86, 165 in the same work, and especially *Mirrour of Justices* (Washington, 1903), pp. 50-51.

[22] Laws of King Cnut (1017-1035), in *Ancient Laws and Institutes of England*, I, 409.

[23] *Ibid.*, p. 251. Most of the Anglo-Saxon codes, however, provided for the payment of a fine to the king as one of his " rights." *Ibid.*, pp. 382 n., 383, 409, 587, etc.

[24] This work, attributed to Andrew Horne, was written about 1290. Many say that the substance of the *Mirrour of Justices* is older than the Conquest.

[25] *Ibid.*, pp. 246, 248. As related to the principle against self-incrimination, it is recorded that " he hanged Seafaule because he judged Olding to death for not answering." *Ibid.*, p. 246.

dations of the principle against unreasonable search and seizure. Careful consideration, however, should be exercised in according a proper place to that document in the history of the Fourth Amendment. The oft-quoted Article 39 of Magna Carta provides as follows: "No freeman shall be taken or [and] imprisoned or disseised or outlawed or exiled or in any way destroyed, nor will we go upon him nor send upon him, except by the lawful judgment of his peers or [and] by the law of the land." This early "due process" clause has been taken to mean much more than it originally did, because of the general tendency—and indeed the great temptation—to explain what is not altogether familiar in an ancient document with what is familiar in one's own experience.[26] Actually, its general and comprehensive phraseology was aimed at certain definite abuses of power by King John,[27] consisting in the main of his practice of taking the law into his own hands and, without legal judgment of any kind or respect for any form of legal procedure whatever, proceeding with or sending an armed force to punish by imprisonment or seizure of property or worse, some person who displeased or disobeyed him.[28] The object of the provision was to prevent in the future all such *extra-legal* procedure, to affirm the validity of feudal law and custom against arbitrary caprice and the indiscriminate use of force,[29] and to prohibit constituted authority from placing execution before judgment.[30]

But here were some roots, these broad generalities in favor

---

[26] William S. McKechnie, *Magna Carta* (Glasgow, 1905), p. 456.
[27] *Ibid.*, p. 437. See the same author, "Magna Carta, 1215-1915," in *Magna Carta Commemoration Essays* (H. E. Malden, ed., Aberdeen, 1917), p. 10.
[28] F. M. Powicke, "Per Iudicum Parium Vel Per Legem Terrae," *ibid.*, p. 103; McKechnie, p. 451; John Lingard, *History of England* (London, 1849), II, 355-356; Reeves, II, 41 n.
[29] See Sir Paul Vinogradoff, "Clause 39," in *Magna Carta Commemoration Essays*, pp. 78-95.
[30] This type of justice was illustrated in the ancient tradition quoted by McKechnie, p. 437:

> I oft have heard of Lydford law,
> How in the morn they hang and draw,
> And sit in judgment after.

of law and liberty, out of which could grow the constitutional maxims of later centuries. They pointed in the direction of the more definite principles which were to develop and they provided imposing precedent and respectable argument for their establishment. Coke and other eminent authorities assumed, perhaps honestly, the existence in some part of Magna Carta of a warrant for every legal principle established in their own day. Moreover, the veneration with which Coke's learning was viewed secured the acceptance of his opinions as to exactly what was meant by the more or less uncertain provisions,[31] although these very errors of Coke and others were of incalculable service to the cause of constitutional progress.[32] " By discovering precedents for a desired reform in some obscure passage of Magna Carta," writes McKechnie, " a needed innovation might be readily represented as a return to the time-honored practice of the past." [33] From this viewpoint more than from any other, the Great Charter may be regarded as important in the background of the principle of reasonable search and seizure. Chapter 39 was relied upon in the arguments and decisions which did much to establish the right as one of constitutional law. It was cited, for example, by James Otis in his famous argument against writs of assistance,[34] by Chief Justice Pratt in *Huckle* v. *Money*,[35] and by Lord Mansfield in *Money* v. *Leach*.[36] These cases will be discussed more fully a little later on.

---

[31] *Ibid.*, p. 447. McKechnie, in *Magna Carta Commemoration Essays*, pp. 12, 19. Cf. James Fitzjames Stephen's comment on the Bill of Rights of 1688 in his *History of the Criminal Law of England* (London, 1883), I, 412.

[32] George B. Adams, *Origin of the English Constitution* (New Haven, 1912), pp. 242-244.

[33] McKechnie, in *Magna Carta Commemoration Essays*, p. 11. See also William Holdsworth, *History of the English Law* (3d ed., London, 1926), IX, 104.

[34] *Paxton's Case* (1761), Josiah Quincy, *Reports of Cases Argued and Adjudged in the Superior Court of Judicature of the Province of Massachusetts Bay, 1761-1772* (Boston, 1865), pp. 51 ff.

[35] 2 Wils. 205, 95 Eng. Rep. 768 (1763).

[36] 3 Burr., 1692, 1742, 97 Eng. Rep. 1050, 1075, *State Trials*, XIX, 1001 (1765). But Madison, in the debate in the first Congress on the occasion of his proposing and sponsoring a bill of rights, stated: " Magna Carta does not contain any one provision for the security

During the Anglo-Norman period, as was the case with the Anglo-Saxon period, just what the rule was which governed official search and seizure within the law is a question upon which hardly any information seems to be available. There is little reason to believe, however, that the authorities, in those cases where official search was necessary, were hampered by any of the limitations and safeguards which we have today.[37] It is most probable that the official badge or commission was sufficient warrant, in everyday administration of the criminal law, for any action of this kind, and that the written warrant was a later development.[38]

However, the objection and resistance of the English people to general inquisitorial methods and their attendant abuses were early reflected in the important statute passed in 1360 in the reign of Edward III, pertaining to powers of justices of the peace. " The King will," the act provided, " that all general inquiries before this time granted within any seignories, for the mischiefs and oppression which have been done to the people by such inquiries, shall utterly cease and be repealed." [39]

---

of those rights, respecting which the people of America are most alarmed." *Annals of Congress*, 1st Cong., 1st sess., p. 453. Cf. F. J. Stimson, *Law of the Federal and State Constitutions* (Boston, 1908), p. 45; H. D. Hazeltine, " The Influence of Magna Carta on American Constitutional Development," in *Magna Carta Commemoration Essays*, pp. 215 ff. On the subject of Magna Carta as related to this discussion, see also *Mirrour of Justices*, chap. v, sec. 2 (p. 262); *ibid.*, p. 293; Holdsworth, I, 60 ff. For Coke's generally discredited exposition of Article 39, see his *Institutes of the Laws of England* (London, 1671), I, 45 ff.

[37] Once in a while, the excesses of minor officials would occasion a demand for reform. For examples of unwarranted seizures of property and of orders that satisfaction be made to those damaged and that in the future *express* authorization should be necessary, see Britton, who wrote about 1300 (translation by F. M. Nichols, Washington, 1901, p. 77). See also, Stephen, I, 81, on the " Inquest of the Sheriffs " in 1170; 3 Hen. VIII, ch. 12.

[38] See Stephen, I, 189 ff.

[39] 34 Edw. III, ch. 1 (1360). The practice of issuing general commissions of inquiry, such as for the arrest of all suspected of having committed a certain type of criminal offense, and imprisonment until further order, was prevalent during this period. Imprisonment of two or three years pending trial was not extraordinary. *Select Cases before the King's Council, 1243-1482* (I. S. Leadam and J. F. Baldwin, edd.), " Selden Society Publications " (Cam-

The legislative history of search and seizure in England may be traced back to the first half of the fourteenth century. Beginning with the early statutes and running down to those enacted in the latter part of the seventeenth century, legislation of this character seems to have been uniformly characterized by the granting of general and unrestricted powers. It was not until the close of this period that a consciousness that such authority was arbitrary and inconsiderate of the liberties of the subject began to filter into parliamentary legislation. This reaction was probably influenced in large measure by the development of more modern ideas in the common law, as we shall see presently.

The first act which comes to attention was passed in 1335. It provided that innkeepers in passage ports were to search guests for false money imported and were to be rewarded with one-fourth of any resulting forfeiture. Official searchers in turn were to search the inns to check up on the innkeepers and receive the same reward for discovery.[40] It may be stated, parenthetically, that still another statute was found necessary in 1402 to regulate abuses in turn among the searchers of the customs.[41]

In the reign of Henry VI (1422-1461), the king granted the Company of Dyers in London the privilege of searching

bridge, 1918), XXXV, p. xl. See also *ibid.*, pp. liii, xc, xcii, civ ff., 59, 83, 85, etc.; 27 Edw. III, St. I, ch. 3 (1352).

Discussing the principle which holds general warrants to be illegal, Stimson remarks: " It is, of course, closely connected with the right of a person not to be compelled to give self-incriminating evidence, but it has a far broader historical connection with the general objection of the Englishman to inquisitions, visitatorial expeditions by king or crown officer, going straight back, indeed, to the great clause of Magna Carta." *Federal and State Constitutions*, p. 45.

[40] 9 Edw. III, St. II, ch. 11. See also chapters 9 and 10 passed at the same session.

[41] 4 Hen. IV, ch. 21. The act prohibited the farming of offices, the occupying of them by deputy, and the acceptance of *douceurs* from merchants.

The general authority and the method of remuneration were in themselves an open avenue to oppression. But the statute indicates in addition the existence of a practice by which the searcher delegated his wide powers to one of his own choosing. See Otis' argument in the Writs of Assistance Case in 1761, charging a like practice in colonial Massachusetts, see below, page 60 n. As to the farming of the customs, see 15 Char. II, ch. 11 (1663).

for and seizing cloth dyed with logwood.[42] This was probably the origin of the practice which was subsequently adopted by Parliament and the Court of Star Chamber, of giving general searching powers to certain organized trades in the enforcement of their sundry regulations. Thus, in 1495, Parliament gave the Mayor of London and the wardens of shearmen in London authority "to enter and search the workmanship of all manner of persons occupying the broad shear, as well as fustians of cloth."[43] A few years later, in the time of Henry VIII, a statute gave the governing authorities of every city, borough, or town, and the masters and wardens of tallow-chandlers, "full power and authority to search for all manner of oils brought in to be sold, in whose hands they be, and as often as the case shall require," with the right to condemn and destroy all altered oils and to commit and punish the persons violating the act.[44]

With the enforcement, in the Elizabethan and Stuart periods, of oppressive laws concerning printing, religion, and seditious libel and treason, the history of search and seizure runs into a broader channel. In 1566, the Court of Star Chamber enacted the first of its famous ordinances in aid of both the licensing of books and the restrictions upon printing established by injunctions, letters patent, etc., regulations which an abundance of evidence shows could never be properly enforced.[45] The Star Chamber, in conformity with the

[42] Richard Thomson, *Historical Essay on the Magna Charta* (London, 1829), p. 226; *Select Cases*, p. cxi (introd.).

[43] 11 Hen. VII, ch. 27. The act 39 Eliz., ch. 13 (1597) provided that since the Mayor of London was too busy to make search with the wardens, the same authority was granted to the master and wardens of the clothworkers or to such "discreet persons" as the latter might appoint.

[44] 3 Hen. VIII, ch. 14 (1511).

[45] The licensing of books had already been decreed by the Queen's Injunctions of 1559, for which see G. W. Prothero, *Select Statutes and Constitutional Documents* (Oxford, 1913), p. 188.

Many patents issued to cover the printing of the best paying books were violated by the poorer printers. In 1560, the Queen's Printer was beginning to make his long series of complaints concerning infringement of his patents. See *Calendar of State Papers (Dom.), 1547-80*, p. 167; John R. Dasent (ed.), *Acts of the Privy Council* (New Series, London, 1895), X, 169, 188, 240, 287. For various cases brought by patentees before the Star Chamber, see

practice mentioned above, decreed that the wardens of the Stationers' Company [46] or any two members deputed by them should have authority to open all packs and trunks of papers and books brought into the country, to search in any warehouse, shop, or any other place where they suspected a violation of the laws of printing to be taking place, to seize the books printed contrary to law and bring the offenders before the Court of High Commission.[47] This was followed in 1586 by another Star Chamber decree which recited that the various laws and ordinances to regulate printing had been totally unheeded and ineffective and provided for stricter censorship, more rigorous penalties, and similar unlimited powers of search and seizure.[48] It would seem that resistance to such search under the older ordinance had not been unusual. This is indicated by the fact that it was now found necessary to insert an additional provision severely punishing any opposition to this authority.

In the same period, great zeal was being shown by the Privy Council and its closely related Courts of Star Cham-

---

Edward Arber, *Transcript of the Registers of the Company of Stationers of London* (Birmingham, 1894), II, 753-806.

[46] For the history of this organization (incorporated in 1556) and the press, see Holdsworth, VI, 362 ff.

[47] Arber, II, 751 ff.; J. R. Tanner, *Tudor Constitutional Documents* (Cambridge, 1922), p. 246; Prothero, p. 168. The records of the Stationers' Company furnish an interesting and amusing illustration of a search undertaken under this ordinance. Thomas Purfoot and Hugh Singleton, members of the company, instituted a long and continuous search, as evidenced by the large expense item which they incurred and which the company paid. This search resulted in the fining of a number of printers for violation of the law. Following the enumeration of these fines, it is recorded that Purfoot, pursuant to a decree of the preceding year for some violation, had to pay a fine that was even greater in amount than the expenses of the search and had to provide also a very heavy bond as surety for future compliance with the law. Evidently those apprehended in his investigation had turned Queen's evidence and had raked up an old decree against Purfoot that might otherwise have been unenforced. Arber, I, 347-348. That the searchers carried with them a written authority is attested by the fact that the Company paid for engrossing copies. *Ibid.*, p. 346. For further details, see *ibid.*, pp. 107b-108b; II, 5a, 5b.

[48] *Ibid.*, pp. 807 ff.; Tanner, pp. 282-283. Cf. the draft act drawn up by William Lambard, the great common law authority of the time, in 1577 and 1580. Arber, II, 751 ff.

ber and High Commission in the detection and punishment
of non-conformism, of seditious libel, and parallel offenses.[49]
No limitations seem to have been observed in giving messengers powers of search and arrest in ferreting out offenders
and evidence. Persons and places were not necessarily specified, seizure of papers and effects was indiscriminate, everything was left to the discretion of the bearer of the warrant.[50]
Oath and probable cause, of course, had no place in such
warrants, which were so general that they could be issued
upon the merest rumor with no evidence to support them
and indeed for the very purpose of possibly securing some
evidence in order to support a charge. To cite one example,
a Privy Council warrant was issued in 1596 for the apprehension of a certain printer, upon information " which maye
touche " his allegiance, with authority to search for and seize
" all bookes, papers, writinges, and other things whatsoever

---

[49] The supervision which the Court of Star Chamber thus exercised led to the assumption of jurisdiction by this tribunal even in
ordinary libel cases. These cases could have been tried in the regular courts but prosecuting officials for good reasons chose to proceed
in Star Chamber. According to Lord Camden (in *Entick* v. *Carrington, State Trials*, XIX, 1067 ff.), it was because of this practice
that there were no libel cases in the Court of King's Bench before
the Restoration.

[50] The records of the Privy Council are full of such instances, of
which the following are examples: A letter to the Knight Marshal
directing him to go to the house of Sir George Peckham " and there
to searche for all manner of letters and papers that may concern the
State," etc. (Dasent, XII, 291); a letter requiring certain persons
to go to the house of an author already under arrest, " to make
searche for all letters, bookes or writings whatsoever that may concern in your judgmentes matter that hath been or may be intended
to be moved in Parliament, and especially suche notes, collections,
books or papers as containe matter touching the establishment of the
Crowne of England," with power to break doors, locks, etc. (*ibid.*,
XXI, 392); a warrant to apprehend certain priests by searching in
any place suspected, and to seize *all* their letters, papers, and writings (*ibid.*, XXIV, 328). Deference to female temperament by the
Council may be seen perhaps in an entry in 1615 that there had been
issued a " generall warrant directed to all his Majesty's publique
officers." It recited that a certain Lady Packington had gone to
London for a visit and had sent up several trunks of clothing which
had been " carried aside " and detained. All officials were ordered
to make search in all places directed by her ladyship. *Ibid.*, XXXIV,
427. For other illustrations see *ibid.*, X, 25; XII, 23, 26, 318; XXI,
403, 409; XXII, 446; XXIV, 399; XXVIII, 120; *Calendar of State
Papers (Dom.), 1547-80*, p. 524; *ibid., 1581-90, passim.* Compare
with these the case reported in Dasent, XXII, 15, 18, 90, 103.

that you shall find in his house to be kept unlawfully and offensively, that the same maie serve to discover the offense wherewith he is charged." [51]

Because of its inordinate character, another instance must be presented to illustrate the methods, as they are related to our study, of such institutions as the Court of Star Chamber in their attempts at law enforcement. In order to apprehend those responsible for certain objectionable and allegedly libellous posters, that tribunal in 1593 issued a warrant to three messengers authorizing them to search for and arrest every person suspected of the libels,

and for that purpose to enter into all houses and places where any such shall be remaining. And, upon their apprehension, to make like search in any of the chambers, studies, chests, or other like places for all manner of writings or papers that may give you light for the discovery of the libellers. And after you shall have examined the persons, if you shall find them duly to be suspected, and they shall refuse to confess the truth, you shall by authority hereof put them to the torture in Bridewell, and by th'extremity thereof, to be used at such times and as often as you see fit, draw them to discover their knowledge concerning the said libels. We pray you herein to use your uttermost travail and endeavor, to th'end the authors of these seditious libels may be known, and they punished according to their deserts. And this shall be your sufficient warrant. [52]

This precept was inspired by Archbishop Whitgift, member of the Privy Council, Star Chamber, and High Commission, who had drafted the decree of 1586 for the censorship of printing, and who was then at the height of his career in suppressing Puritan dissent. [53] The same warrant, incidentally, had an intimate connection with the death of Christopher Marlowe. [54]

---

[51] *Ibid.*, XXVI, 425.

[52] Quoted in C. F. Tucker-Brooke, *Works and Life of Christopher Marlowe* (New York, 1930), pp. 54 ff.

[53] *Ibid.*, pp. 55-56; Tanner, p. 246. For Whitgift's participation in searches for papists and in the case of the famous Martin Marprelate libels, see John Strype, *Life and Acts of John Whitgift* (London, 1822), I, 182 ff., 232, 551-601, *passim*.

[54] One line of investigation under this warrant led to the arrest on the following day of Thomas Kidd, whose papers were searched in the manner desired by the Privy Council. Certain heretical works discovered there were imputed by Kidd to Marlowe and this resulted in an inquiry by the Council into Marlowe's atheism. For the connection of this inquiry with his death soon afterwards, see the

The reign of James I did not set a much better example. Arbitrary powers were again granted freely in the continued persecution of non-conformists, in the censorship of the press, and in statutes for the regulation of trade.[55] In addition, the authorities were beginning to use the writ or warrant of assistance, a general search warrant which was later to become so famous. This warrant was found to be of convenient use in the customs service and developed during this time from the similar practice of the Privy Council. This fact, incidentally, may properly be emphasized at this point. Writers and jurists have shown no acquaintance with the existence of the writ of assistance as of such an early date but have assumed its creation by a statute of 1662 for the better enforcement of the customs laws. For example, in the case of *Cooper* v. *Boot*,[56] it was a material factor in the case

---

interesting article by Ethel Seaton, " Marlowe, Robert Poley, and the Tippings," *Review of English Studies*, 1929, V, 274 ff.

[55] See the various documents in Prothero, pp. 370, 394-396, 424 ff., 427. See also the following statutes: 1 Jac. I, ch. 19, sec. 3; 3 Jac. I, ch. 4, sec. 35; 3 and 4 Jac. I, ch. 5, sec. 15; 7 Jac. I, ch. 4.

Laws in regulation of religion were enforced by the Court of High Commission and apposite remarks concerning the functioning of that body, although the facts presented are of a slightly later period, might be presented at this point. In 1634 there were issued from that tribunal *circulars* to all peace officers directing them to search *every room* of any house where they should have intelligence that non-conformist services were being held, to arrest all persons there assembled, and to seize all unlicensed books. Such general warrants, of the broadest possible kind, were very usual throughout these times, warrants which Stephen writes were wholly illegal even according to existing laws, for they authorized the arrest and imprisonment, merely upon suspicion, " persons who by law were not liable to be imprisoned at all even upon conviction, except upon a significavit from the Court of King's Bench and a writ *de excommunicato capiendo*."

The oppression which these warrants must have caused is indicated by a petition which the keeper of a certain prison submitted to the Court of High Commission. After detailing his past success in discovering such offenders and hoping for " better service in that kind hereafter," the keeper requested that he be favored by the Court and that more of these prisoners should be committed into his custody. The petition pleased the tribunal and the keeper was rewarded for his good work with the order that the offenders should be committed " now and then " to his prison, where, of course, they were a source of profit to him. In this manner, his zeal to continue his patriotic and conscientious service in behalf of both church and state was no doubt still further inspired. See Stephen, II, 426 ff.

[56] 4 Doug. 347 (1785).

whether the writ existed independently of this statute. The question was specifically put to counsel by Lord Mansfield, but although the case was postponed in order that an inquiry might be made, no earlier trace of the writ was reported found.[57] Yet, in 1621, a member of Parliament was already recommending that such warrants should not be issued so frequently.[58]

The attempted rule of Charles I by prerogative alone was naturally productive of even more outstanding instances of arbitrary action of interest in this discussion. In the first few years of this reign the question of general warrants had already come into prominence. These, however, were not of the type considered above. They were mandates, on the other hand, to arrest and imprison *named* persons upon the mere fiat of the king—" *per speciale mandatum domini regis* "— similar to the *lettres de cachet* of French history. They were general in the sense that no definite legal offense was charged against the person except that he had incurred the displeasure of the monarch.[59] These precepts were used with convenience in 1627 to imprison those who would not pay the " forced loan " levied by Charles I to fill his empty treasury after Parliament had refused to grant him the necessary appropriations. Upon habeas corpus, the court held that the

---

[57] See also the monograph by Horace Gray, Jr., on writs of assistance, in Quincy, pp. 530 ff.

[58] A quotation in Edward Channing, *History of the United States* (New York, 1912), III, 5 n., gives the clue to this fact of the early existence of the writs, but the source there cited (*Proceedings and Debates of the House of Commons, 1620-1621*, p. 225) does not make it entirely clear whether the reference was to search warrants used by customs officers or to other distinct types of legal process also known as writs of assistance which were used in Chancery or in the Exchequer. However, all doubts on this question are dispelled by an item in a manuscript which the present writer chanced upon in the *Fourth Report of the Historical Manuscripts Commission* (London, 1874), p. 312. In the list of the Earl de la Warr collection, the following appears: " July 30, 1621—Copy of Council Order, that the Lord Treasurer may make Warrants of Assistance for suppressing the importation and sale of Tobacco except by the Undertakers, and the Constables may break into any shop or place suspected." The development of this type of warrant in the Privy Council may be traced in Dasent, XXXIV, 588, 672; XXXV, 321; XXXVI, 407; XXXVII, 56; XXXVIII, 423, 449. 452, 465, 479.

[59] Cf. the Sixth Amendment to the United States Constitution.

justification in the return, namely, that the king had so willed, was sufficient.[60] Those imprisoned were later released but the damage had already been done. The storm that had long been brewing from this and other causes now broke upon the king. The Parliament of 1628, to which were elected many of those who had been imprisoned as just described, forced him to sign the Petition of Right, calling for the cessation of this procedure of committing persons " without any cause showed ." and other practices as contrary to Magna Carta and the laws of England.[61]

The year following, the king attempted to collect the duty of " tonnage and poundage," a clear violation of law and indeed of the Petition of Right itself, since Parliament had refused to grant the tax.[62] The people resisted and employed numerous devices to avoid payment, whereupon the government resorted to the use of violence, the seizure of goods, and the imprisonment of the merchants to enforce satisfaction of the tax. The Privy Council gave orders, moreover, empowering its messengers to enter into any vessel, house, warehouse, or cellar, search in any trunk or chest and break any bulk whatsoever, and arrest anyone making any speech against his Majesty's service or causing any disturbance. An historian of the period writes that these officers under pretense of searching " used many oppressions and rogueries, which

[60] *Darnell's Case, State Trials*, III, 1 ff. Cf. the Opinion of the Judges (1591), in Holdsworth, V, 497-499.

[61] For the long history of this type of warrant and comment thereon, see McKechnie, pp. 458-459; Powicke, in *Magna Carta Commemoration Essays*, pp. 113 ff.; Holdsworth, V, 191; VI, 32 ff. Cf. William Lambard, *Justices of the Peace*, pp. 95-96; *Parliamentary History of England* (W. Cobbett, ed.), II, 260 ff.

With reference to the search and seizure provision of the Massachusetts Bill of Rights adopted in 1780, it has been remarked in an article on the sources of that document that, as regards the stipulation governing seizure of the person, relation was undoubtedly had to these events which had made a deep impression on the public mind in England in 1627, just before the Massachusetts colonists left for America. E. Washburne, "Massachusetts Bill of Rights," *Massachusetts Historical Society Proceedings, 1864-1865* (Boston, 1866), VIII, 312-313. See also the first article of the Massachusetts Body of Liberties of 1641, in Francis Bowen, *Documents of the Constitution of England and America* (Cambridge, 1854), p. 58.

[62] Holdsworth, VI, 42 ff., 70.

caused the people still more to exclaim." [63] The final and natural result of all these arbitrary measures, characteristic of all attempts at law enforcement in the teeth of public feeling, was that the king had little revenue and the people were more dissatisfied than ever.

General search for documentary evidence was also a prevalent practice during Charles' rule. Privy Council warrants, for example, were issued in 1629 for the searching and sealing of the trunks, studies, cabinets, and other repositories of papers of such leading personages as John Selden and Sir John Elliot after their insurrectionary speeches in Parliament on the levying of tonnage and poundage without the consent of Parliament. [64] They were subsequently committed along with others " during the king's pleasure " for their seditious actions and language, upon warrants similar to those in use before the Petition of Right, although the return upon habeas corpus was more specific. [65] But the most outstanding of these instances was the case of Sir Edward Coke, the celebrated authority on the common law and most influential of the Crown's opponents. On the theory that certain works in preparation contained matter prejudicial to the prerogative, that seditious papers were in circulation among the popular party, and that this was an opportune time to discover them and to strike a telling blow, the Privy Council in 1634, when Coke was on his deathbed, sent a messenger to his home with an order to search for " seditious and dangerous papers." Practically all of his writings, including the manuscripts of his great legal works, his jewelry, money, and other valuables, and even his will, were seized under that warrant and carried away. His chambers at the Inner Temple were ransacked in the same manner. The havoc wrought by the custodians of these papers was wanton, [66] and

---

[63] Paul de Rapin-Thoyras, *History of England* (London, 1747), II, 285. His statement, however, that these search powers had never been practiced before is, of course, subject to criticism. See also the paper presented to the king in 1629 by the Bishop of London, in John Rushworth, *Historical Collections* (London, 1722), II, 8-9.

[64] *Ibid.*, I, 665 ff.   [65] *State Trials*, III, 235 ff., 313.

[66] Cuthbert W. Johnson, *Life of Sir Edward Coke* (London, 1837),

seven years elapsed before what remained was restored to his heirs at the request of the Long Parliament. His will, of great importance to his family, was never returned.[67]

In 1637, the Star Chamber issued another ordinance placing a still stricter censorship upon everything printed. Searchers were given authority in even more blanket terms than before and, lest any doubt exist as to whether there were any limitations of propriety upon the general powers usually conferred, *express* provision was made this time that they could search at any time of the day or night they saw fit.[68]

But with the upheaval in English politics beginning with the assembling of the Long Parliament in 1640, certain steps were taken, at the outset at least, that seemed to augur well for the cause of liberty. The Court of Star Chamber which, notwithstanding the high opinion of contemporaries [69] and its development of certain departments of substantive law,[70] has left a black name in history because of the methods it employed, was abolished, along with its associated tribunal, the Court of High Commission.[71] The year following, the House of Commons resolved that the searching and sealing of the studies and papers of the members of Parliament in 1629 and the issuance of warrants for that purpose had been a

---

II, 320 ff. For a catalogue of the property seized, see *ibid.*, pp. 323-329.

[67] See Humphrey W. Woolrych, *Life of Coke* (London, 1837), pp. 189 ff.; Holdsworth, V, 454-455, with citations to original sources; W. H. Lyon and H. Block, *Edward Coke* (Boston, 1930), pp. 329-330.

[68] Arber, IV, 534-535; Rushworth, III, 313-314.
The system of licensing which was enacted is interesting. Law books, for example, had to be licensed by the lord chief justice or the lord chief baron, books on history by the secretaries of state. Hale stipulated in his will that none of his manuscripts should be printed after his death, for fear of changes which might be made by the licensers.

[69] See the opinions of Coke, Bacon, and others in Prothero, pp. 175, 180 ff., 401, 408.

[70] For a comprehensive survey of its work and influence by a present-day authority, see Holdsworth, V, 178-214.

[71] 16 Char. I, ch. 10; 16 Char. I, ch. 11. The Privy Council, however, was still permitted to retain the power of examining and committing persons charged with offenses, provided that on habeas corpus the jailer would certify the true and specific cause of imprisonment. The court then examined the legality and justice of the complaint.

breach of privilege on the part of those who executed the warrants, for which they were to be punished.[72] One of the grounds of impeachment of the Earl of Strafford was that he had granted to a certain bishop and his subordinates a general warrant of arrest.[73]

However, as is more or less typical of human nature, once this Parliament had become firmly seated in power, it adopted and permitted measures that were no more heedful of the liberty of the individual than were those of the preceding régime. In 1643 an ordinance for the regulation of printing continued the severe censorship and allowed equally broad discretionary powers of search in enforcing its provisions.[74] It was this ordinance which caused Milton to write his *Areopagetica,* pleading for a free press. Moreover, in the prosecution of disaffected persons the same arbitrary methods usual in the reign of Charles were employed by some of the very men who had in such righteous manner inveighed against

---

[72] Rushworth, I, 665 ff.; *State Trials.* III, 310 ff. See the various speeches on grievances in 1640 in *Parliamentary History*, especially II, 641, 649, 658. See also the proceedings in the House of Lords relating to the search of the studies and pockets of the Earl of Warwick and Lord Brook and the seizure of their papers as a breach of privilege on the ground that the warrants *did not specify any particular act* (*ibid.*, pp. 667 ff.) ; and the case of Lord Kimbolton and others referred to in Somers' *Collection of Tracts* (London, 1810), IV, 342-343.

[73] *State Trials,* III, 1391. In the colony of Virginia there was passed in 1643 what was probably the first legislative precedent of the Fourth Amendment, prohibiting the issue of blank warrants. Hening, *Statutes at Large*, I, 257-258, cited in a German dissertation on the Virginia Bill of Rights by Gustav A. Salander, *Vom Werden der Menschenrechte* (Leipzig, 1926), p. 58. The abuses of this practice, however, had been recognized even in England and the Privy Council had ordered in 1631 that no more blank warrants should be presented by the clerk for signature, an indication of the presence and probable abuse of the practice beforehand. Edward R. Turner, *The Privy Council* (Baltimore, 1928), I, 199. And the Star Chamber had fined a justice of the peace for issuing blank warrants, with name and offense to be filled in later. Michael Dalton, *Justice of the Peace* (London, 1746), p. 402.

[74] *Acts and Ordinances of the Interregnum* (C. H. Firth and R. S. Rait, edd., London, 1911), I, 185-186. This ordinance was followed by a number of other regulations to promote enforcement, giving authority of search to a great variety of persons. See Ordinance of 1647, *ibid.*, I, 1022; Act of 1649, *ibid.*, II, 247-248, 251; Act of 1652-53, *ibid.*, p. 698.

these methods at that time.[75] A new form of tax, the excise, was invented and imposed to raise funds for the war against Charles, carrying with it an unlimited authority of invasion of private homes with which this tax was always later identified by the people.[76]

To be sure, the activities of the excise officers soon provoked remonstrances from a public opinion which was becoming more and more sensitive to arbitrary practice and more alive to what *ought to be* the right of the individual.[77] This growing consciousness was in line with what the judges were doing in developing the common law, as will be seen presently. If it was wrong for a sheriff to do a certain thing, what right had an excise or other officer to do the same thing?

Let us then inquire into the state of development of the common law at this period with regard to search and seizure. English jurisprudence it seems had begun to shape itself along more modern lines and conceptions of liberty and justice. The principle that search and seizure must be reasonable, that there must be a balancing of the problems of the administration of justice with those of the freedom of the individual, was emerging slowly and was assuming more and more the character of an underlying concept of jurisprudence.[78] However, before this principle could definitely and

---

[75] For example, Prynne, the champion of liberty who himself objected to general powers in excise officers, searched the study of Archbishop Laud and seized his private papers and books. Certain of these were needed for the latter's defense but, although restitution was promised, only part was returned. Somers, IV, 443.

[76] *Ibid.*, I, 164-165, 207, 282, 667-669. See the criticism of the excise on this ground by Sir William Blackstone in his *Commentaries* (Cooley ed., Chicago, 1876), I, 318 ff.

[77] Many pamphlets appeared, denouncing the excise and the procedure of its enforcement. See citations in William Kennedy, *English Taxation* (London, 1913), p. 62 n. In *Excise Anotomiz'd*, anonymously published in 1659, the writer lists as one of his grievances: " The uncivil Proceedings of the Officers thereof, who, upon every suspicion, and often malicious Information, come into our Houses, with armed men, and if not immediately let in, violently break open our Doors, to the great Affrightment and Amazement of our Wives, Children, and Families." (ed. 1733, p. 15.)

[78] The idea that a man's house was his castle had always continued to play a part in English legal thought. In 1470, for exam-

finally impress and establish itself in the public mind as a fundamental right of *constitutional* importance, the more spectacular situations present in the eighteenth century were necessary.

In a contemporaneous seventeenth-century treatise on the history of the pleas of the crown by Chief Justice Hale, one of the greatest jurists in English history,[79] the chief limitations upon the exercise of search and seizure now embodied in such constitutional provisions as the Fourth Amendment are already found presented either as law or as recommendations of the better practice, which later hardened into law. For instance, a general warrant to apprehend all persons suspected of having committed a given crime was held by Hale to be void and no defense to a suit for false imprisonment.[80] The party asking for the warrant should be examined under oath touching the whole matter, whether a crime had actually been committed and the reasons for his suspicion.[81] The warrant should specify by name or description the particular person or persons to be arrested and must not be left in general terms or in blanks to be filled in afterwards.[82] Upon the reasoning of the first rule, Hale held that warrants to search any suspected place for stolen goods were invalid (although he admitted that there were precedents of such general warrants)[83] and should be restricted to search

---

ple, it was decided that although it was lawful for an owner of goods to enter upon the land of another who had wrongfully taken them from him, he could not break into his house. *Yearbooks*, 9 Edw. IV, Mich. Pl. 10, cited in Holdsworth, III, 279. A constable broke doors to search at his peril in hue and cry. Sir Matthew Hale, *History of the Pleas of the Crown* (Philadelphia, 1847), II, 98-104. A debtor's house was always considered his asylum and could not be broken into. James Paterson, *Commentaries on the Liberty of the Subject* (London, 1877), II, 231 ff. See also *Semaine's Case*, 5 Coke 91 (1604); Francis Lieber, *Civil Liberty and Self-Government* (Philadelphia, 1874), pp. 62-63.

[79] For an evaluation of Hale's work, see Holdsworth, VI, 574-595.

[80] Hale, I, 580; II, 112, citing *Justice Swallow's Case*, P. 24, Car. I.

[81] *Ibid.*, II, 110. Cf. *ibid.*, I, 582. The examination must be put down in writing. *Ibid.*, p. 586.

[82] *Ibid.*, pp. 576-577; II, 112-114.

[83] See an example of such a warrant in the old work by Dalton, pp. 418-419.

in a particular place suspected, after a showing, upon oath, of the suspicion and the "probable cause" thereof, to the satisfaction of the magistrate. "For these warrants," he said, "are judicial acts, and must be granted upon examination of the fact. And therefore, I take these general warrants dormant, which are made many times before any felony committed, are not justifiable, for it makes the party to be in effect the judge; therefore, searches made by pretense of such general warrants give no more power to the officer or party, than what they may do by law without them."[84] It is "convenient," he added, that the precept should express that the search be made in the daytime; that the complainant ought not be given the warrant for execution, although he should be present to give the officer information of his goods; that no doors be broken open; and that the goods should not be delivered to the complainant until so ordered by the court.[85] Coke previously, in a somewhat ambiguous statement, had denied altogether the legality of search warrants for stolen goods.[86] On the question of warrants of arrest "to answer such matters as shall be objected" against the party, Hale wrote that such warrants, notwithstanding earlier precedents

---

[84] Hale, II, 150. See also *ibid.*, p. 79.

[85] *Ibid.*, pp. 113-114, 149-151.

[86] Coke, IV, 176, 177. See Hale's comment, II, 107, 149; James Fitzjames Stephen, *Digest of Criminal Procedure* (London, 1882), p. 81. See also Hale's criticism of Coke on the question of granting warrants of arrest upon suspicion before indictment. II, 79-80, 107-110.

The practical workings of the police system seem to have nullified much of the substantial progress made by the law. This was due to the fact that in those times the justices of the peace combined in their persons the functions of magistrate, policeman, and prosecutor. The oppressive practices of these officials in the 17th century are described in John Pollock, *The Popish Plot* (London, 1903), pp. 267 ff. "They raised hue and cry, chased criminals, searched houses, took prisoners. A Justice of the Peace might issue the warrant for arrest, conduct the search himself, effect the capture, examine the accused, and sans witnesses, extract a confession by cajoling as friend and bullying as magistrate, commit him, and finally give damning evidence on trial." See also Stephen, *History of the Criminal Law*, I, 221 ff.; *State Trials*, VI, 572-575.

of their use, were not regular [87] and anyone so arrested was to be discharged upon habeas corpus.[88]

However, these salutary rules of the common law exercised but little influence upon Parliament. In the first year after the Restoration, it is true, an act to enforce the payment of customs duties did provide for the issuance of special warrants under oath in searches of houses and for full damages and costs against the informer if the information proved to be false.[89] But two years later, several statutes were enacted which were of the same stamp as the legislation of preceding régimes. Incidentally, these statutes were to play leading rôles in the events on both sides of the Atlantic that laid the permanent foundation for the principle of reasonable search and seizure. The first was the Licensing Act for the regulation of the press.[90] It made provision for powers of search as broad as any ever granted by Star Chamber decree. The second was an act " to prevent frauds and abuses in the custom." One instrumentality to aid in its enforcement was the general writ of assistance already mentioned.[91] A third statute passed in the same year brought into existence the hated " hearth money," in the collection of which officials

---

[87] *Ibid.*, I, 577-578, citing Lambard, pp. 95-96; Coke, II,, 591, 615. Dalton gives instances of such warrants by Chief Justice Popham, pp. 401-402.

[88] Hale, II, 111, citing *Brown's Case*, P. 23, Car. B. R. Such warrants had been held good in earlier times in treason and felony cases. *Ibid.* See Coke's argument before the House of Lords in 1628, *Parliamentary History*, II, 260 ff.

[89] 12 Char. II, ch. 19; see also 12 Char. II, ch. 4, sec. 22. But compare other statutes of the same year, 12 Char. II, ch. 22, sec. 5, and 12 Char. II, ch. 23, sec. 19.

[90] 13 and 14 Char. II, ch. 33. The search and seizure provision of the act is section 15.

[91] 13 and 14 Char. II, ch. 11, sec. 5. For further discussion, see pages 53 ff., below. Provision for this general warrant was probably made in order to avoid the inconveniences from the standpoint of enforcement which were involved naturally in the use of the special warrant of 1660. See the opinion of Attorney General de Grey, in Gray, Quincy's *Reports*, pp. 452-454. The argument of James Otis to the effect that these warrants were not originally meant to be general may be found in the succeeding chapter. There is no doubt, however, that the later practice was to issue general writs of assistance by virtue of this statute. Walpole, in *Parliamentary History*, VIII, 1278; Mansfield, C. J., in *Cooper* v. *Boot*, 4 Doug. 347; Opinion of de Grey, cited above.

were given right of entry into all houses any time during the day.[92]

The Licensing Act expired upon the refusal of Charles II to summon Parliament in 1679. In order not to lose the advantages of this legislation, the king called together the twelve judges of England to decide whether the press could be as effectively regulated by the common law as by the statute. The chief justice was Scroggs, always extremely facile in arriving at any opinion agreeable to the Crown. After resolving that seditious libel was a criminal offense at common law and that such libels could be seized, the judges came to the rather remarkable conclusion that to write, print, or publish any book, pamphlet, or other matter, was illegal without a license from the king.[93] A proclamation was accordingly issued by Charles to suppress seditious libels and unlicensed printing and the chief justice, in turn, upon the basis of the proclamation, issued general warrants of search and arrest to enforce it.[94] In 1680, the activities of Scroggs and his associates were investigated by the House of Commons. Printers and booksellers hastened to complain of unjust vexation by the messengers of the press armed with these warrants. When Scroggs was impeached, one of the articles of impeachment was based on his issuance of " general warrants for attaching the persons and seizing the goods of his majesty's subjects, *not named or described particularly*, in the said warrants; by means whereof, many . . . have been vexed, their houses entered into, and they themselves grievously oppressed, contrary to law." [95] Here was a legislative recognition of the

---

[92] 13 and 14 Char. II, ch. 10, sec. 3.

[93] *Harris' Case, State Trials*, VII, 929 ff.; *Carr's Case, ibid.*, p. 1127. See the caustic reference to this opinion by Chief Justice Pratt in *Entick* v. *Carrington, ibid.*, XIX, 1069 ff.

[94] Two of these warrants are set out in *ibid.*, VIII, 192-193.

[95] *Ibid.*, p. 200 (italics mine). First the committee of investigation and then the House of Commons had resolved that these warrants were " arbitrary and illegal." *Ibid.*, pp. 193, 195, 211. Parliament was soon after prorogued and the proceedings against Scroggs dropped. The king later did remove him from the bench, but at the same time every mark of favor was shown him, including the granting of a pension.

It is interesting to note in passing that such considerations as the

idea that general warrants were an arbitrary exercise of governmental authority against which the public had a right to be safeguarded.[96]

After the Revolution of 1688, another forward step was taken in acknowledgment of this privilege. One of the first acts of the new government, by insistance of King William himself, was to abolish " hearth-money." But what is of most interest here is the reason given for this action. The " hearth-money," declares the preamble of the statute, is not only a great oppression of the poorer classes, " but a badge of slavery upon the whole people, exposing every man's house to be entered into, and searched by persons unknown to him." [97] From this time on through the whole succeeding

House of Commons expressed in its resolutions did not prevent the reenactment of the Licensing Act in 1685 and 1692 with provision for general search and seizure. Upon the expiration of the act in 1695, however, it was finally rejected.

[96] Mention might be made here of the infamous trial of Algernon Sidney in 1683, so important in constitutional history generally. The point that is of interest here is that a general warrant contributed to the results reached in that case. The Privy Council sent an order to seize *all* of Sidney's papers and writings. This warrant was carried out to the letter. Under a later warrant his money, valuables, and clothes were seized. Certain private papers that were picked up, in which Sidney had once jotted down remarks unfavorable to the king and which were not meant for publication, were held by the corrupt presiding judge to supply the defect of the second witness necessary in treason cases. G. Van Santvoord, *Algernon Sidney* (New York, 1854), pp. 228 ff. It is stated in a leading work on the American Constitution that this seizure of papers in Sidney's case was very intimately connected with the adoption of the Fourth Amendment itself. See Thomas M. Cooley, *The General Principles of Constitutional Law* (4th ed., Boston, 1931), p. 267; also T. J. Norton, *Constitution of the United States* (Boston, 1922), p. 208. In view of the much more proximate reasons for the Fourth Amendment, however, this statement is entirely too broad.

For other cognate material in the reign of Charles II, see an instance where the king himself censured a too rigorous search of the houses of certain favorites as done " to satisfy the private passion " of the minister responsible. Clarendon to Bagot, *Report of Commission on Historical Manuscripts* (London, 1874), IV, 329. See also *State Trials*, IX, 1005.

[97] 1 Wm. and M., ch. 10. The king played a leading part in this reform. As early as March 1, 1689, he sent a message to Parliament urging the regulation or abolition of this tax as grievous to the people. In the debate thereon, it was brought out that he did this on his own initiative and that nobody had expected it when he made the motion in council saying he was much concerned about the matter. *Parliamentary History*, V, 152-153.

period there may be noticed a certain tendency in legislation not to grant powers of search and seizure as lavishly as had been the case in former years.[98]

Upon occasion, a threatened invasion of this privilege could inflame the public mind in a remarkable manner. This was what happened in 1733 when Walpole proposed his plan, known in history as the Excise Scheme, to tax wines and tobaccos, not as a custom duty upon importation, but after warehousing and as the goods were withdrawn for home consumption. From the standpoint of economics, this project has been declared adequate to establish Walpole as a finance minister far in advance of his day.[99] At the time, however, it excited such popular agitation as to shake his power to its very foundations.[100] The party opposing Walpole, quickly

---

[98] See 1 Wm. and M., ch. 24, levying an excise on liquor, which provided for the same means of enforcement as by 12 Char. II, ch. 19 (the "special warrant" act of 1660 considered above) and 15 Char. II, ch. 11, but significantly omitted the writs of assistance act of 1662. Compare the summary powers granted for the enforcement of the gaming and fishing laws, 3 and 4 Wm. and M., ch. 10, sec. 3; 4 and 5 Wm. and M., ch. 23.

See also 5 Geo. I, ch. 28; 10 Geo. I, ch. 10, sec. 13. In connection with sections 10 and 12 of this last act, however, see the protest of the merchants in 1733 after the success of the opposition to the Excise Scheme. *Parliamentary History*, IX, 9.

[99] See Adam Smith's *Wealth of Nations*, Book V, chap. ii, cited in R. H. I. Palgrave's *Dictionary of Political Economy* (London, 1925), I, 781 ff. But Smith viewed with disfavor "frequent visits and odious examination" of tax collectors, exposing people "to much unnecessary trouble, vexation, and oppression." He was of opinion that this was one of the ways in which a tax frequently became so much more burdensome to the people than it was beneficial to the sovereign and was therefore to be avoided (Cannon ed., London, 1904, II, 312).

[100] *Parliamentary History*, VIII, 1307-1310.

Besides being a tax, and therefore unpopular of itself, the harassing practices associated with the enforcement of the excise and the great number of people who were subjected to the methods employed made this form of taxation and even its very name peculiarly disagreeable to the English people. Johnson so defined the word "excise" in his dictionary that in the opinion of legal authorities it amounted to a libel upon the excise commissioners. Chesterfield, remembering the troubles experienced by Walpole in 1733 and by Bute with the cider tax in 1763, once facetiously remarked concerning a pending measure: "As for a general excise, it must change its name by act of Parliament before it goes down with the people, who know names better than things; for aught I know, if an act for a general excise were to be entitled 'An act for better preserving the liberty and property of his majesty's subjects, by repealing

sensing the opportunity, strongly emphasized both the proposed extension of the unpopular excise laws to additional commodities and the investigation and search provisions of the bill.[101] In vain did Walpole argue that only those places registered as storehouses of tobacco were to be liable at all times to the inspection of the officer, that a special warrant would be necessary to search any other part of the house, and that the customs practice was stronger, since officers there could enter merely by virtue of their writs of assistance, without an affidavit.[102] But the inquisitorial provisions for strict supervision were offensive and he was forced for this and other reasons to withdraw the bill, an action which met with as loud rejoicing, says one writer, as the most glorious national victory ever gained.[103]

Great opposition was likewise aroused in 1763 when the cider tax was passed, extending the excise laws to a commodity which would bring practically everyone into contact with the administration of these laws. William Pitt spoke against it, particularly against the dangerous precedent of admitting officers of the excise into private houses. The laws of excise were grievous to the trader, he said, but intolerable to the private person. The government admitted that the excise was odious but maintained it was necessary. Provisions in the act regarding investigation the government

---

some of the most burdensome custom-house laws,' it might be gladly received." See Stephen Dowell, *History of Taxation in England* (London, 1884), II, 105-107.

[101] See the debates in Parliament over the measure, particularly the statements of Mr. Pulteney and Sir John Barnard on the vexatious practices of excisemen in *Parliamentary History*, VIII, 1299-1300, 1316-1317, with which compare the comment in the note, *ibid.*, p. 1232.

Blackstone, after describing in his *Commentaries* (I, 318 ff.) the economic advantages of the excise, says: " But, at the same time, the rigour and arbitrary proceedings of excise laws seem hardly compatible with the temper of a free nation. For the frauds that might be committed in this branch of the revenue, unless a strict watch is kept, make it necessary . . . to give officers a power of entering and searching the houses of such as deal in exciseable commodities at any hour of the day, and in many cases, of the night likewise. . . ."

[102] *Parliamentary History*, VIII, 1278.

[103] *Ibid.*, IX, 8; Dowell, II, 106.

justified on the ground that they were much more lenient than in the case of hop-growers who, so the argument ran, often had their very bedchambers visited by the exciseman. In the House of Lords a number of protests were filed by dissenting members "because by this Bill our fellow subjects, who from the growth of their own orchards, make Cyder and Perry, are subjected to the most grievous mode of excise; whereby private houses of peers, gentlemen, freeholders, and farmers are made liable to be searched at pleasure." [104] Disturbances broke out in the cider counties and troops had to be moved into them. London and many other corporations and counties petitioned against the act and especially against its visitation provisions. The tax had to be repealed several years later, coincidental with the resolution of the House of Commons concerning general warrants.[105]

Probably arising out of the practice under the Licensing Act and inadvertently continued when that act failed of re-enactment, a usage had grown up for the secretary of state to issue general warrants of search and arrest in seditious libel and similar cases. Strange to say, in all the years between the rejection of the statute in 1695 and the accession of George III in 1760, the validity of these warrants was questioned only once, and then more or less casually. In that instance, in the case of *Rex* v. *Earbury*,[106] the warrant had directed the seizure of *all* the defendant's papers, but Lord Hardwicke had refused to give an opinion on the point on the ground that since he had no authority to order the return of the papers, the question was not before the court.[107] But it was this continued exercise of power that was destined to lead to the final establishment of the principle of

---

[104] *Parliamentary History*, XV, 1307-1316.

[105] William Hunt, *History of England, 1760-1801*, "The Political History of England" (William Hunt and Reginald L. Poole, edd.), X (London, 1905), 43-44, 72.

[106] 2 Barn. K. B. 396, 94 Eng. Rep. 544 (1733).

[107] Earlier in the same year, when he was still attorney general and not yet on the bench, Hardwicke had argued with Walpole that the broad powers of search and seizure in enforcing the customs and excise laws were not unreasonable. *Parliamentary History*, VIII, 1289. Compare his position in 1763 on the cider tax, *ibid.*, XV, 1311-1312.

reasonable search and seizure upon a constitutional footing in England and to constitute at the same time one of the main factors in the history of such provisions in American bills of rights.

In 1762, John Wilkes, then a member of Parliament, began to publish anonymously his famous series of pamphlets called the *North Briton,* deriding the ministers and criticizing the policies of the government. This continued until the following year when *Number 45* of this series appeared, containing an unusually bitter attack upon the King's Speech in which, incidentally, among other things, the cider tax had been highly praised.[108] Smarting under the constant and effective censure, the government determined to apprehend and prosecute the responsible party and by the usual procedure. A warrant was issued by Lord Halifax, the secretary of state, to four messengers, ordering them " to make strict and diligent search for the authors, printers, and publishers of a seditious and treasonable paper, entitled, The North Briton, No. 45, . . . and them, or any of them, having found, to apprehend and seize, together with their papers."

Here was a warrant, general as to the persons to be arrested and the places to be searched and the papers to be seized. Of course, probable cause upon oath could necessarily have no place in it since the very questions as to whom the messengers should arrest, where they should search, and what they should seize, were given over into their absolute discretion. Under this " roving commission," they proceeded to arrest upon suspicion no less than forty-nine persons in three days,

---

[108] The King's Speech (recognized, of course, as that of his ministers) had lauded the unpopular Peace of Paris and also, due to the riots in the cider districts, had called for a spirit of concord and obedience to law which were essential to good order. The *North Briton,* Number 45, retorted: " Is the *spirit of concord* to go hand in hand with the PEACE and EXCISE, through this nation? Is it to be expected between an insolent EXCISEMAN, and a *peer, gentleman, free holder, or farmer,* whose private houses are now made liable to be entered and searched at pleasure? " *The North Briton* (London, 1772), II, 256; see also *ibid.,* Number 43, p. 205.

Asked once by Madame Pompadour how far the liberty of the press extended in England, Wilkes replied: " I do not know. I am trying to find out." Raymond Postgate, " *That Devil Wilkes* " (London, 1930), p. 53.

even taking some from their beds in the middle of the night.[109] Finally, they apprehended the actual printer of *Number 45* and from him they learned that Wilkes was the author of the pamphlet. Wilkes was waiting for just such an opportunity, having on different occasions advised others to resist such warrants.[110] He pronounced the messengers' authority " a ridiculous warrant against the whole English nation " and refused to obey it. The messengers thereupon took him up in a chair and conveyed him in that manner to the office of the secretary of state, after which, accompanied by an undersecretary of state, they returned to the house. Refusing admission to any of Wilkes' friends, they had a blacksmith open the drawers of Wilkes' bureau and took away, uninventoried, all of his private papers including his will and also his pocketbook. Wilkes afterwards was committed to the Tower by the secretary of state upon his refusal to answer questions but was released a few days later upon habeas corpus by reason of his privilege as a member of Parliament.

All the printers, upon the suggestion and with the. support of opponents of the government, brought suit against the messengers for false imprisonment. Chief Justice Pratt held the warrant to be illegal. " To enter a man's house by virtue of a nameless warrant," said the Chief Justice, " in order to procure evidence, is worse than the Spanish Inquisition; a law under which no Englishman would wish to live an hour." The London jury awarded the particular plaintiffs in the test cases damages of £300 and the other plaintiffs had verdicts of £200 by consent.[111]

---

[109] Dryden Leach, a printer who had worked on other numbers of the pamphlet but not this one, was arrested during the night, together with his employees, and all of his papers seized. The messengers did this on the following information: " Mr. Carrington, the messenger, told three other messengers, who executed the warrant, that he had been told by a gentleman, who had been told by another gentleman, that Leach's people printed the paper in question." Nuthall to Pitt, July 7, 1763, in *Correspondence of William Pitt* (W. S. Taylor and J. H. Pringle, edd., London, 1838), II, 230.

[110] See Postgate, pp. 57-58.

[111] See *Huckle* v. *Money*, 2 Wils. K. B. 206, 95 Eng. Rep. 768 (1763). The defendants asked for a new trial on the ground that

Wilkes brought suit against Wood, the undersecretary who had superintended the execution of the warrant. The Chief Justice this time upheld a verdict of no less than £1000 in favor of the plaintiff. He declared that this warrant was a point of the greatest consequence that he had ever met with in his whole practice.

The defendants claimed a right under precedents to force persons' houses, break open escritoires, seize their papers, upon a general warrant, where no inventory is made of the things taken away, and where no offenders' names are specified in the warrant, and therefore a discretionary power given to messengers to search wherever their suspicions may chance to fall. If such a power is truly invested in a secretary of state, and he can delegate this power, it certainly may affect the person and property of every man in this kingdom, and is totally subversive of the liberty of the subject. If higher jurisdictions should declare my opinion erroneous, I submit as will become me, and kiss the rod; but I must say I shall always consider it as a rod of iron for the chastisement of the people of Great Britain.[112]

A suit by Leach, a printer, against the messengers brought him a verdict of £400. Wilkes got a judgment of £4000 against Lord Halifax himself a number of years later. The government undertook the responsibility of defending all actions arising from the warrant and the payment of all judgments. The expenses incurred were said to total £100,000.[113]

These decisions were greeted with the wildest acclaim all over England. " Wilkes and Liberty " became the byword

---

the verdict was excessive. But Pratt, after admitting that £20 would have been sufficient for the imprisonment of six hours, went out of his way with a bit of novel reasoning to sustain the verdict: " But the small injury done to the plaintiff, or the inconsiderableness of his station and rank in life did not appear to the jury in that striking light which the great point of the law touching the liberty of the subject appeared to them at the trial; they saw a magistrate over all the king's subjects, exercising arbitrary power, violating Magna Carta, and attempting to destroy the liberty of the kingdom, by insisting on the legality of this general warrant before them; they heard the King's Counsel, and saw the solicitor of the Treasury endeavor to support and maintain the legality of the warrant in a tyrannical and severe manner. These are the ideas which struck the jury on the trial; and I think they have done right in giving exemplary damages."

[112] *Wilkes* v. *Wood*, Lofft 1; 98 Eng. Rep. 489; *The North Briton*, III, 42-43.

[113] See in general T. E. May's *Constitutional History of England* (Boston, 1864), II, 245-252.

of the times, even in far-away America.[114] Chief Justice
Pratt became one of the most popular men in the country.
He was given addresses of thanks in large numbers and presented with the freedom of London, Dublin, and other cities.
The city of London requested, in addition, that he sit for
his portrait for the famous artist, Sir Joshua Reynolds.
When completed, the portrait was hung in Guildhall with an
inscription by Dr. Johnson, designating him the " zealous
supporter of English liberty by law." [115] Pratt's opinions on
the question of general warrants, moreover, were directly responsible for his subsequent elevation to the peerage in 1765
and to the lord chancellorship in 1766.[116]

The government appealed the Leach case to the Court of
King's Bench. The case came up before that court two years
later. Judgment for the plaintiff was affirmed but, because
the facts of the particular case did not render it necessary
to go further, the actual decision was made to turn on the
point that since the warrant had authorized the arrest of the
authors, printers, and publishers of the *North Briton, Number 45,* and of them only, the defendants could not in any
event justify under it when they arrested persons who were
in no way involved in the publishing of *Number 45.* The
judges, however, went on to give their opinion of the validity
of the warrant itself and in this they agreed fully with the
views of Pratt. " A usage to grow into law," held Chief
Justice Mansfield, " ought to be a general usage, one which
it would be harmful to overthrow after a long continuance.
This on the other hand, was a usage of a particular office,

---

[114] In the famous elections of 1768 and later, when Wilkes was
repeatedly elected to and expelled by the House of Commons, one of
the chief grounds of his candidacy was his conduct with regard to
general warrants. See *The North Briton,* III, 155, 158, 195, 199.
His correspondence with leading Americans in this period was also
considerable. See Postgate, chap. x, especially the address to Wilkes
signed by James Otis, Samuel Adams, John Hancock, John Adams,
and Josiah Quincy, among others (p. 193).

[115] Edward Foss, *Judges of England* (London, 1870), p. 536. His
portrait became the favorite sign of public-houses throughout the
country, William E. H. Lecky, *History of England in the Eighteenth
Century* (London, 1882), III, 79-80.

[116] See the very interesting material in Basil Williams' *Life of
William Pitt* (London, 1913), II, 158 ff.

and contrary to the usage of all other justices and conservators of the peace. . . . It is not fit that the judging of the information should be left to the officer. The magistrate should judge, and give certain directions to the officer." Mr. Justice Wilmot thought the warrant "illegal and void," and the two other judges, Yates and Anson, had no doubt of its illegality, "for no degree of antiquity can give sanction to a usage bad in itself." [117]

In November of 1762, a half year before the *North Briton* incident, Lord Halifax had issued a warrant to the messengers to search for John Entick, author of the *Monitor or British Freeholder,* and seize him together with his books and papers. This warrant was specific as to the person but general as to papers. The messengers in this instance also, as might be expected, made the most of the discretion granted them. Entick at first took no action, but after witnessing the success of Wilkes and the printers, he was encouraged to sue the messengers in trespass for the seizure of his papers.[118] The jury gave him a verdict of £300 damages.

This case was later argued before the Court of Common Pleas. In 1765, Pratt, now Lord Camden, delivered the opinion of the court,[119] an opinion which has since been denominated a landmark of English liberty by the Supreme Court of the United States.[120] "If this point should be decided in favor of the Government," said the court, "the secret cabinets and bureaus of every subject in this kingdom would be thrown open to the search and inspection of a messenger, whenever the secretary of state shall see fit to charge, or even to suspect, a person to be the author, printer, or publisher of a seditious libel." An unreasonable power, the court went on, must have a specific foundation in law in order to

---

[117] *Money* v. *Leach*, 3 Burr. 1692, 1742, 97 Eng. Rep. 1050, 1075, *State Trials*, XIX, 1001 (1765). See the extended argument of de Grey, who at that time was solicitor general, attempting to uphold the warrant. *Ibid.*, pp. 1016 ff.

[118] Dr. Birch to Lord Royston, in George Harris, *Life of Lord Chancellor Hardwicke* (London, 1847), III, 368.

[119] *Entick* v. *Carrington, State Trials*, XIX, 1029 (1765).

[120] *Boyd* v. *United States*, 116 U. S. 616, 6 Sup. Ct. 524, 29 L. ed. 746 (1886).

be justified. A person's "house is rifled," the court continued, "his most valuable papers are taken out of his possession, before the paper, for which he is charged, is found
to be criminal by any competent jurisdiction, and before he
is convicted of writing, publishing, or being concerned in the
paper. Such is the power, and therefore one should naturally expect that the law to warrant it should be as clear in
proportion as the power is exorbitant." The origin of the
practice was in Star Chamber days; the Licensing Act had
expired; and the usage since the Revolution of issuing these
warrants, not based upon any statutory authority, was abso-
lutely illegal. The court, sarcastically referring to the old
tribunal consisting of Scroggs and his associates as "a great
and reverend authority," denied that they could by their
extrajudicial resolution establish in law the general search
warrant which, indeed, was so soon thereafter condemned by
the House of Commons. To the argument of long usage the
court answered: "There has been a submission of guilt and
poverty to power and the terror of punishment. But it would
be a strange doctrine to assert that all the people of this land
are bound to acknowledge that to be universal law, which a
few criminal booksellers have been afraid to dispute." [121]

The subsequent resolutions of the House of Commons with
respect to general warrants were largely a result of these
two circumstances, the opinions of the judges in the recent
cases and the popular feeling on the question. None of the
law officers of the Crown defended the legality of the warrant in the course of the parliamentary debate. Charles
Yorke, who had been attorney general at the time the warrant was issued, actually protested its legality during the
discussion and maintained that he had not been consulted
on that question. But to Pitt goes the actual credit of forc-
ing the hand of the Commons in the matter. In February,
1764, when the question was brought up on the floor of the
House, he was the central figure in the debate. All that the
Crown and the ministers had desired, he declared, had been

---

[121] *Entick* v. *Carrington*, cit. above. The opinion in 2 Wils. 275
is a shorter report.

accomplished in the conviction of Wilkes for libel and his expulsion from Parliament. Now it was the duty of Parliament to do justice to the nation, the constitution, and the law. He denied that precedent afforded any justification. He himself, as secretary of state, had issued similar warrants in 1760, not in mere libel cases, but in cases of emergency arising from the state of war. He knew them to be illegal because his friend Pratt, who was then attorney general, had told him they would be illegal and that he would have to take the consequences. But "preferring the general safety, in time of war and public danger, to every personal consideration, he ran the risk, as he would of his head, had that been the forfeit, upon the like motive."[122]

The government succeeded in postponing the decision on the question only by the barest majority. Two years later, in April, 1766, the House of Commons resolved that general warrants in cases of libel were illegal. But this limited condemnation did not satisfy Pitt. He forced the House to declare that general warrants were universally invalid, except as specifically provided for by act of Parliament, and if executed upon a member of the House, a breach of privilege. But an attempt to introduce a bill to prohibit the seizure of persons by general warrants was turned down. And a bill to restrain the issuance of warrants to seize papers, except in cases of treason and felony without the benefit of clergy, and then under certain regulations, which was passed by the Commons, was rejected by the House of Lords.[123]

One of Pitt's many eloquent remarks on these occasions, a sample of his great oratorical powers, has become classic:

The poorest man may, in his cottage, bid defiance to all the forces of the Crown. It may be frail; its roof may shake; the wind may

---

[122] *Parliamentary History*, XV, 1401-1403; *Correspondence of William Pitt*, II, 288.

Most of the groundwork of Pitt's classic arguments in Parliament was also furnished by Pratt. A secretary of state, Pratt told him, could no more issue general warrants than any other magistrate since there was no difference between state crimes and other crimes; they were all to be prosecuted, judged, and punished by the same common and equal law, the law books admitting no such things as the French *raison d'état*." See Williams, II, 157-158.

[123] *Parliamentary History*, XVI, 207 ff.

blow through it; the storm may enter; the rain may enter; but the
King of England may not enter; all his force dares not cross the
threshold of the ruined tenement.[124]

In this manner did Pitt express the consummation of the
ideal " a man's house is his castle," the subordination of governmental authority to the principle of safeguarded search
and seizure.[125]

---

[124] Quoted in Thomas M. Cooley, *A Treatise on Constitutional
Limitations* (8th ed., Boston, 1927), I, 611.

[125] The *lettres de cachet* of French history have also been mentioned in connection with the Fourth Amendment. See *United States
v. Innelli*, 286 Fed. 731 (1923); John E. F. Wood, " Scope of Constitutional Immunity Against Searches and Seizures," *West Virginia
Law Quarterly*, 1928, XXIV, 1. It may be recalled that the violent
outcry by the French people against these warrants was more or less
contemporaneous with the adoption of the American bills of rights.
However, the *lettres* seem to be more closely related to the provisions of the Sixth Amendment which guarantee to an accused a
public trial, the right to be informed of the nature of the accusation against him, to be confronted with the witnesses against him,
and the right to counsel. See also page 29, above. There were a
number of different types of these warrants, but the one that is of
interest here is that by which the king sentenced a subject to possibly lifelong imprisonment without the privilege of a trial and the
opportunity for defense. The search for and seizure of evidential
papers or other things were not necessary since this was a final com-
mitment and did not require any substantiation in fact to support it.
The *lettres* did not charge any criminal offense and sometimes were
issued in blank, the name of the person to be arrested being filled in
by some functionary. Besides the injustices inherent in the *lettres*
themselves, many abuses were naturally prevalent in their administration. The practice was abolished by the Constituent Assembly as
demanded by the *cahiers* of 1789 and was the source of repeated
protest and a factor in the causes of the French Revolution.

A facsimile of a *lettre de cachet* is in Frantz Funck-Brentano, *Les
lettres de cachet* (Paris, 1926), p. 7. A leading work on the subject
is André Chassaigne, *Des lettres de cachet sous l'Ancien Régime*
(Paris, 1903).

The Code of Offenses and Punishments in 1793 provided that
searches and seizures had to take place in the presence of the
accused, if arrested, and that the latter was entitled to furnish expla-
nations, identify the objects seized, and initial seals. A. Ésmein,
History of Continental Criminal Procedure (Boston, 1913), p. 506.

CHAPTER II

WRITS OF ASSISTANCE IN THE COLONIES

On this side of the Atlantic, the argument concerning the validity of general search warrants centered around the writs of assistance which were used by customs officers for the detection of smuggled goods. Contemporaries generally accepted it as a fact, and historians agree, that the controversy on this question which took place in Massachusetts in 1761, the first serious friction between the British customhouse officers and the colonists, was " the first in the chain of events which led directly and irresistibly to revolution and independence." [1] In order to get a proper view of this interesting episode, however, it is necessary to digress for a moment into more or less familiar history by way of background.

In the first place, the British Government had enacted various trade regulations and restrictions with regard to the American Colonies to further the policy of protecting England's own industries and commerce. One of these enactments, the Molasses Act of 1733, is particularly important in the present connection. In order to protect the British West Indies, which Great Britain chose to regard as more useful economically than the Colonies, this act laid a prohibitive duty upon the importation of molasses and sugar from the non-British West Indies.[2] But the prosperity of the northern colonies depended upon the important rum distilling industry. In the colony of Rhode Island alone it was estimated that the distilleries needed 14,000 hogsheads of molasses annually, whereas the British West Indies could

---

[1] Albert Bushnell Hart, in *American History Leaflets*, No. 33, Introduction. George Bancroft writes that John Adams, Governor Bernard, and Chief Justice Hutchinson all agree, especially the latter in his correspondence, that Otis' argument in the Writs of Assistance Case was the origin of the party of revolution. *History of the United States* (Boston, 1852) IV, 416 n. See also George L. Beer, *British Colonial Policy, 1754-1765* (New York, 1907), p. 123; Eben G. Scott, *Development of Constitutional Liberty in the English Colonies of America* (New York, 1882), pp. 245-246, 299 ff.

[2] William S. McClellan, *Smuggling in the American Colonies* (New York, 1912), pp. 43 ff.

supply only about 2,500.[3] The French and Spanish islands, on the other hand, could adequately supply the indispensable amount of molasses. At the same time, they furnished an excellent market for such leading industries as fishing and lumber and thus provided a source of capital wherewith the colonists could cover the trade balance which was favorable to England and pay for the manufactured goods they were forced to import from the mother country because of the prohibitions upon colonial manufacture.[4]

The unfairness of the Molasses Act was recognized even in England. It was enforced in lax fashion, evaded universally, and merchants resorted to petty bribery of customs officials. This situation seems to have been disregarded by the home government and the act was renewed every five years notwithstanding.[5] The natural trade with the non-British West Indies gradually became so extensive and important that its curtailment meant commercial disaster for the Colonies.[6] After the outbreak of the Seven Years War, the benefits of this trade to the French made it necessary for England to bring it to an end. In 1760, accordingly, orders were given for the strict enforcement of the trade laws.[7] Thus a form of smuggling which, because of its long existence and sufferance had come to be considered as almost legal trade, became smuggling in a very real sense.[8]

---

[3] James Truslow Adams, *Revolutionary New England* (Boston, 1923), p. 294; Channing, *History of the United States*, III, 3. Cf. the Declaration of Rights and Grievances drawn up by the Stamp Act Congress, of which James Otis was a leading member, in 1765, especially Articles 9 to 11. See also Adam Smith's criticism of British policy in his *Wealth of Nations*, quoted in Marion M. Miller, *American Debate* (New York, 1916), I, 6.

[4] See McClellan, chaps. iii-v, for an informative survey of the commercial problems confronting the Colonies.

[5] *Ibid.*, pp. 47, 88; Beer, p. 231; J. T. Adams, p. 295.

[6] McClellan, p. 92.

[7] For a copy of Pitt's instructions to the authorities in America, see Gray, in Quincy, *Reports of Massachusetts Bay, 1761-1772*, pp. 407-408.

The news that the Molasses Act was to be enforced " caused greater alarm in this country than the taking of Fort William Henry did in 1757," wrote Governor Bernard. Adams, p. 293.

[8] The amount of duties collected from 1760 on shows that the Molasses Act was enforced to an extent unknown theretofore. Beer,

From the standpoint of the more effective enforcement of these trade laws, the convenience of general search warrants was very apparent.[9] As pointed out in the preceding chapter, provision had been made for such warrants in like instances in England by the act of Charles II passed in 1662,[10] by virtue of the broad terms of which any person who was authorized by a writ of assistance [11] under the seal of the English Court of Exchequer could take with him a civil officer and search any house, shop, warehouse, etc.; break open doors, chests, packages, in case of resistance; and remove any prohibited or uncustomed goods or merchandise.[12] Furthermore, an act of William III passed in 1696 contained the broad stipulation that the officers of the customs in America were to be given " the same powers and authorities " and the " like assistance " that officials had in England.[13]

These writs, which received their name from the fact that they commanded all officers and subjects of the Crown to

---

pp. 115-116. The statement has been made that if from the time of its enactment the Molasses Act had been rigorously enforced by writs of assistance, it is not unlikely that the Revolution would have been hastened by 30 years. George E. Howard, *Preliminaries of the Revolution* (New York, 1905), p. 83. The economic and political background of this period is presented in the following works: George L. Beer, *British Colonial Policy, 1754-1765* (1907), the most authoritative treatment of the subject, especially from the economic standpoint; Marcus W. Jernegan, *The American Colonies* (New York, 1929), chap. x; Hunt, *Political History of England*, X, chap. v, *passim*; William J. Ashley, *Surveys Historic and Economic* (London, 1900), pp. 309-360. Compare Gerald B. Hurst, *Old Colonial System* (Manchester, 1905), pp. 70 ff., who presents the English viewpoint; Adams, pp. 209-296, especially pp. 269-273.

[9] Justin Winsor, *Narrative and Critical History of America* (Boston, 1884), VI, 11.

[10] 13 and 14 Char. II, ch. 11, sec. 5 (1662).

[11] Sometimes spelled " writ of assistants." See the point made as to this by Gridley in the November argument. Quincy, pp. 56-67.

[12] See the commentary on Otis' argument that these warrants should be construed as special, by Gray, in Quincy, pp. 530 ff. But the fact remains that the practice in England was to the contrary, notwithstanding Otis' assertion that the recent practice in England made the writs returnable. Otis cited a London magazine as his authority. Thomas Hutchinson, *History of the Colony of Massachusetts Bay* (Boston, 1828), III, 93-94; Johnson to Pitkin, April 29, 1768, *Massachusetts Historical Society Collections* (5th ser., Boston, 1885), IX, 292. Cf. note 20, below.

[13] 7 and 8 Wm. III, ch. 22, sec. 6 (1696).

assist in their execution,[14] were even more arbitrary in their
nature and more open to abuse than the general warrants of
the *North Briton* cases.[15] The warrants in those cases, it is
true, authorized the apprehension of undescribed persons and
the indiscriminate seizure of their papers, but they were connected with a particular case of libel and consequently were
necessarily limited to some extent not only in object, but
what is more important, in time. In other words, the warrants were not permanent in the officers' hands to be used
thenceforth to search for and seize the authors of *all* seditious
libels and their papers. The more dangerous element of the
writ of assistance, on the other hand, was that it was not returnable at all after execution, but was good as a continuous
license and authority during the whole lifetime of the reign-
ing sovereign. The discretion delegated to the official was
therefore practically absolute and unlimited. The writ empowered the officer and his deputies and servants to search,
at their will, wherever they suspected uncustomed goods to
be, and to break open any receptacle or package falling under
their suspecting eye.[16] Its only redeeming features were
that it did not of itself authorize the arrest of anyone and
that it permitted the search of land structures only in the
daytime.[17] It was also necessary that a civil officer be present

---

[14] This was not the objectionable feature. Incidentally, the assistance of bystanders may now also be asked in the execution of search
warrants. See 18 U. S. C. A., sec. 614.

The assistance required even of a sheriff only extended to seeing
that the officers were protected and assisted in the discharge of their
duties and not to assistance in unloading cargo or unrigging vessels,
as customs officers apparently had requested of one sheriff at least.
Hutchinson's opinion in Gray, in Quincy, pp. 464-465. Disobedience
of the writ was a contempt of court.

[15] For a copy of the writ, see *ibid.*, pp. 404, 418 ff.; William Mac-
Donald, *Documentary Source Book of American History* (New York,
1908), p. 106. A facsimile of the only original writ of assistance
extant is in Frederic A. Ogg, *Builders of the Republic* (New Haven,
1927), p. 39.

[16] The statute of 1662 provided for the breaking open of chests,
trunks, etc., only in case of resistance. The writs issued in Massachusetts, especially the earlier ones, were so loosely worded as to omit
specifications of even this restriction.

[17] The writ stipulated that vessels could be searched both during
the day and night, without a civil officer.

but this was a precaution which was of doubtful value except possibly to the customs officer himself.[18]

Most of the events concerning these writs of assistance in America took place in the province of Massachusetts Bay.[19] The early practice of customs officials there and elsewhere had been to enter buildings forcibly by the mere authority of their commissions as officers. This procedure, legally un-justified in the case of English officials but probably not con-sidered extraordinary in early times, as indicated by enact-ments in Massachusetts with respect to provincial collectors, seems to have been unopposed for a long period of time. Later on, however, the people did grow uneasy and began to resist or sue the officers, so that in the administration of Governor Shirley the expedient was adopted by the governor of issuing general writs of assistance.[20] After these writs had

---

[18] Compare Gridley's argument, Quincy, pp. 56-67. See note 76, below.

[19] The best account of writs of assistance in the Colonies is the excellent and painstaking work by Horace Gray, Jr. (later Chief Justice of Massachusetts and Justice of the United States Supreme Court), which constitutes Appendix I of Quincy's *Reports of Massachusetts Bay, 1761-1772*, pp. 395-540. This must be supplemented by a paper entitled "Malcom and Writs of Assistance," *Massachusetts Historical Society Proceedings, 1924-1925*, LVIII, 5-84. General accounts may be found in any standard history of the period, among which may be listed Channing, III, 3-5, 93, 95, 114; Claude A. Van Tyne, *Causes of the War of Independence* (Boston, 1922), pp. 176 ff.; Howard, pp. 73-83; Scott, pp. 237-248, 299 ff.; William B. Weeden, *Economic and Social History of New England* (Boston, 1890), II, 671 ff.; William Tudor's *James Otis* (Boston, 1823), pp. 53-90; John G. Palfrey, *History of New England* (Boston, 1890), V, 235-243; George R. Minot, *History of Massachusetts Bay* (Boston, 1803), II, 87-99; Henry Belcher, *First American Civil War* (London, 1911), I, 78 ff.

[20] See Hutchinson, III, 92, for his comment on this practice of Shirley's. See also Beer, p. 123; Gray, in Quincy, pp. 401 ff.

An examination of the Maryland Archives reveals a colonial writ of assistance of an earlier date than any the writer has seen men-tioned before. This writ was issued by the Council of Maryland to Patrick Mein, Surveyor General of the Customs in Virginia and Maryland, on November 10, 1686, in response to his request for a writ of assistance "as is usual in such cases." The writ, however, did not recite any general powers of search and its sole purpose was to command assistance, but the fact is evident that the recitation in Mein's commission of general search powers was taken by everyone concerned to be of itself sufficient authority in this regard. Indeed, the commission itself reads like a general writ of assistance. *Archives of Maryland* (Baltimore, 1887), V, 521-524.

Besides the fact of the early date, this material is interesting in

been in use for several years, this irregularity too, namely, their issuance by the governor himself, was brought to his attention, whereupon he directed the officers to apply for them to the Superior Court of the province. In 1755, the Superior Court granted a writ to Charles Paxton, the Surveyor of the Port of Boston, and thenceforth continued to exercise the function.

But the objection to general warrants as such had not as yet been manifested by the colonists. Indeed, from 1748 to 1756, the Massachusetts legislature itself had provided that collectors of provincial duties and deputies appointed by these collectors had the right to search wherever their suspicion directed for wines and spirits upon which the local duty had not been paid.[21] At the first session of the legislature, however, after Paxton received his writ from the Superior Court, this law was changed so as to make special warrants requisite.[22]

In 1760, a number of occurrences took place which resulted in making 1761 a memorable year not only in the present discussion but in American history as well. First of all, there was appointed to the governorship of Massachusetts Bay Sir Francis Bernard, who was a dependable Crown officer. Then, soon afterwards, Chief Justice Sewell of the

---

several respects. First, it seems to demonstrate that in those early times and for a long time afterwards the officers were permitted to search any time and any place upon the sole authority of their commissions, and that at an early date after the passage of the statute 13 and 14 Char. II (1662) the writ of assistance itself was not looked upon as any authorization of general search. Second, the statute passed in 1672 cited in Mein's commission for his right of general search (25 Char. II, ch. 7) does not appear to give any such power. Third, the date of the incident was ten years before the statute 7 and 8 Wm. III, which purported to give the same authorities to the customs officers in America that those in England had. The general power to search in the commission, accordingly, does not seem to have been based upon any legislative sanction but only upon the authority of the customs administration.

[21] Adams, p. 271, citing *Acts and Resolves of the Province of Massachusetts Bay* (Boston, 1878), III, 406, 471, 522, 581, 622, 701, 762, 845. These acts did not even provide for the general warrants which Adams states were authorized.

[22] *Acts and Resolves*, III, 1008-1009. For later years, see *ibid.*, IV, 186, 303, 411, cited in Beer. See also Prov. St. 32 Geo. II, ch. 1 (1758).

Superior Court died. Now, in the absence of opposition, Sewell had granted writs of assistance to the customs officers, but it is an important fact that he was reputed to have had doubts as to their legality. The leading candidate for the position was the liberal-minded James Otis, Sr., of Barnstable, an eminent lawyer of the province, who had been promised the first vacancy by former Governor Shirley.[23] But Governor Bernard naturally was desirous of having a court that would support the Crown in any controversy, so he appointed to the post Thomas Hutchinson, the Lieutenant Governor of the province, to the disappointment of Otis and his son James Otis, Jr., who was later to become a leader in the movement for independence.[24] Hutchinson thus held two positions which were really inconsistent.[25] He was a man of honest intentions but of illiberal and unpopular views, a merchant and not a lawyer.[26]

Then, on October 25, George II died. Conformably to a statute of Anne, all writs of assistance expired six months after the death of the sovereign. And the stage was finally set when in the same year Pitt gave instructions for the strict enforcement of the trade laws.

In February of 1761, all writs of assistance expired. Sixty-three Boston merchants immediately petitioned the court for a hearing on the question of granting new writs.[27] The

---

[23] William Gordon, *History of the American Revolution* (New York, 1801), p. 100.

[24] Hutchinson himself throws some light on the governor's zeal, in this remark in his diary: " The Governor was very active in promoting seizures for illicit trade, which he made profitable by his share in the forfeitures." Peter O. Hutchinson, *Diary and Letters of Thomas Hutchinson* (London, 1883), I, 67. For charges of corruption against Bernard, see Gray, in Quincy, p. 424 n.

[25] Hutchinson was also councillor and judge of probate. Bancroft, IV, 379.

[26] Hutchinson, after his appointment, makes the following statement in his diary (he wrote in the third person) : " This employment engaged his attention, and he applied his intervals to reading the law; and though it was an eyesore to some of the Bar to have a person at the head of the law who had not been bred to it, he had reason to think the lawyers in general at no time desired his removal." Hutchinson, *Diary*, I, 66.

[27] The fact that the commerce of Connecticut and Rhode Island was unhampered by customs officers who did nothing to enforce the

merchants were represented by the younger Otis, who had resigned the lucrative position of advocate general in order to avoid arguing in favor of the writs,[28] and Oxenbridge Thatcher, a prominent liberal of Boston. The customs officers were represented by Jeremiah Gridley, attorney general of Massachusetts Bay.[29]

Gridley relied on the statute of 1602 providing for writs of assistance to be issued by the English Court of Exchequer, the statute of William broadly giving customs officers in America the same powers as in England, and a provincial statute which gave to the Superior Court the jurisdiction of the English Courts of Exchequer, King's Bench, and Common Pleas.[30] He argued that the court was bound by these acts to issue the writs. " If it is the law in England," he maintained, " it is the law here. It is extended to this country by Act of Parliament." The power given by the writ was no greater infringement of English liberties than constables distraining for rates, he claimed, and necessity justified both measures.[31]

But Otis completely electrified the large audience in the court room with his denunciation of England's whole policy toward the Colonies and with his argument against general warrants.[32] John Adams, then a young man less than twenty-

---

law had quite a bit to do with the opposition in this and other instances by the Boston merchants. Beer, pp. 117-118; J. T. Adams, p. 293.

[28] Gray writes: " The charge commonly made by the supporters of prerogative against James Otis, that his subsequent public course was dictated solely in revenge for his father's disappointment may be classed with D'Israeli's insinuation that John Hampden's refusal to pay ship-money was occasioned by an ancient grudge against the sheriff who levied it." Quincy, p. 411.

[29] Benjamin Prat, who was about to leave for New York to become Chief Justice there, was solicited by both sides but declined. He was a spectator at the trial of the case. Tudor, p. 56.

[30] Prov. St. 11 Wm. III (1699).

[31] Gray, in Quincy, pp. 57, 469, 477.

[32] The current elaborated version of Otis' argument may be found in Charles Francis Adams, *The Life and Works of John Adams* (Boston, 1856), II, 523-527; Minot, II, 87-99; Albert Bushnell Hart, *American History Told by Contemporaries* (New York, 1901), II, 375 ff.; M. C. Tyler, *Literary History of the Revolution* (New York, 1897), I, 30 ff. Primary sources of the arguments are the notes taken by John Adams at the first trial of the case in February (*Works of*

six years of age and not yet admitted to the bar, was a spectator, and many years later described the scene in these oft-quoted words: " I do say in the most solemn manner, that Mr. Otis's oration against the Writs of Assistance breathed into this nation the breath of life." [33] He " was a flame of fire! Every man of a crowded audience appeared to me to go away, as I did, ready to take arms against Writs of Assistance. Then and there was the first scene of opposition to the arbitrary claims of Great Britain. Then and there the child Independence was born. In 15 years, namely in 1776, he grew to manhood, and declared himself free." [34]

Otis contended that since general warrants were not sanctioned by the common law, the writ of assistance mentioned in the act of 1662 should be construed as special like the writ of assistance provided for in the earlier act passed in 1660,[35] especially since the later statute did not give a clear definition of the writ.[36] If this statute, passed in the reign of Charles II when arbitrary power was pushed to an extremity, *did* authorize general warrants, then, he maintained, it was unconstitutional, repugnant to Magna Carta. And foreshadowing the great principle of American constitutional law, he argued that an act against the Constitution, on the authority of Lord Coke in *Dr. Bonham's Case,*[37] was void.

Here was an instrument that appeared to him " the worst instance of arbitrary power, the most destructive of English liberty, that ever was found in an English law book." Even the old general warrants for stolen goods issued by justices of the peace had been made special in modern times. This was

---

John Adams, II, 521-523; Gray, in Quincy, pp. 469-477) and Josiah Quincy's own report of the second argument in November (*ibid.*, pp. 51-57). Unfortunately, the latter was absent during the greater part of Otis' speech on that occasion. For a discussion of the evolution of the present version, see Samuel A. Green, " Otis against the Writs of Assistance," *Massachusetts Historical Society Proceedings, 1890, 1891* (2d Ser.), VI, 190 ff.

[33] *Works of John Adams*, X, 276.

[34] *Ibid.*, pp. 247-248.

[35] 12 Char. II, ch. 19. See page 37, above.

[36] See note 12, above.

[37] 8 Coke's Rep. 107, 118 (1609). See Gray's interesting discussion of this and other points in Quincy, pp. 512-540.

a power that placed the liberty of every man in the hands of every petty officer. Anyone with this general warrant could be a tyrant and reign secure in his petty tyranny. That a man's house was his castle was one of the most essential branches of English liberty, a privilege totally annihilated by such a general warrant. Customhouse officers were given permission to enter houses when they pleased. They and their deputies might break open everything in their way, and if they broke from malice or revenge, no man could inquire, since bare suspicion without oath was sufficient. He related how Mr. Justice Walley had called Mr. Ware before him by a constable to answer for some minor offense. " As soon as he had finished, Mr. Ware asked him if he had done. He replied, ' Yes.' ' Well then,' said Mr. Ware, ' I will show you a little of my power. I command you to permit me to search your house for uncustomed goods.' And went on to search his house from the garret to the cellar; and then served the constable in the same manner." [38]

The vivid description of the whole case by John Adams fifty-seven years afterwards may have been somewhat colored and his memory of details imperfect,[39] but the impression which the event made upon him was not a mere illusion of a senile mind. Otis' speech moved him profoundly and brought him to a sharp awakening. The observation has been made that this impression made by Otis upon Adams

---

[38] " Mr. Pew had one of these writs, and when Mr. Ware succeeded him, he endorsed this writ over to Mr. Ware; so that these writs are negotiable from one officer to another." This charge by Otis brings to Gray's mind a case that arose in 1860. The sergeant-at-arms of the United States Senate endorsed over to another person a precept to arrest one who had refused to appear before a Senate committee. The witness was arrested but ordered released by the Supreme Judicial Court of Massachusetts on the ground that this procedure was invalid. *Sanborn* v. *Carlton*, 15 Gray 399. The Judiciary Committee of the Senate opposed this decision and reported a bill giving such power to the sergeants-at-arms of the Senate and House, but the bill was not passed. Quincy, pp. 475-476 n.

[39] Between the years 1815 and 1818, Adams devoted a great deal of his correspondence to establishing the fame of Otis, especially as regarded his part in the Writs of Assistance Case. *Works*, X, 183, 233, 244, 247, 272, 276, 292, 314, 317, 338, 362. For criticism of his account, see *ibid.*, p. 362 n.; Quincy, p. 469 n.; Ashley, pp. 356-357.

was the former's greatest contribution,[40] a somewhat extreme but not altogether idle remark. It is usually overlooked that in the very midst of the first few days of July, 1776, just at the moment that "the child Independence," to use Adams' phrase, had grown to manhood, when Adams was taking the leading part in putting through the Second Continental Congress the resolution of independence, he fittingly recalled and gave a merited importance to the incident which had done much to inspire his career. "When I look back to the year 1761," he wrote to his wife on the morning of July 3, 1776, communicating the news of the action of Congress in passing the resolution, "and recollect the argument concerning writs of assistance, in the superior court, which I have hitherto considered as the commencement of the controversy between Great Britain and America, and recollect the series of political events, the chain of causes and effects, I am surprised at the suddenness of this revolution." [41]

But the comparatively neglected argument of Thatcher is also important, both from the legal and historical standpoints. This is especially so in the light of several documents which a recent investigation of the papers in the Treasury files of the Public Record Office in London has unearthed.[42] Thatcher maintained that according to the express wording of the statute of 1662, there could be only one valid general writ of assistance, if any, and that was one issued from, and under the seal of, the English Court of Exchequer; that Parliament, in providing for this writ had given one court, and one court only, the power to issue it. He argued that aside from this and notwithstanding the fact that the provincial statute gave the Superior Court the juris-

---

[40] Frank P. Grinnell, "John Winthrop and the Constitutional Thinking of John Adams," in *Massachusetts Historical Society Proceedings, 1929-1930*, LXIII, 98, 107, 115-116.

[41] Quoted in Mabel Hill, *Liberty Documents* (New York, 1901), pp. 188-189.

[42] See below, pp. 64 ff. This new material is the result of the enterprising research of Mr. George G. Wolkins, and was presented in 1924 to the Massachusetts Historical Society in a paper entitled "Malcom and Writs of Assistance," *Massachusetts Historical Society Proceedings*, LVIII, 5-84.

diction of the Court of Exchequer, the Superior Court had in
a number of instances disclaimed the powers possessed by the
English court. And his conclusion was that the statute of
William III providing generally for the same powers and
authorities for the customs officers in America that those in
England had, did not bridge the gap sufficiently to take the
place of the express stipulation of the statute of 1662 which
specifically lodged the power in the English Court of Exchequer.[43] In other words, his argument was to the effect
that although the statute of William III when considered
abstractly seemed to extend the availability of the general
writs to the Colonies, yet, precisely, it had failed to provide
the court for and consequently the mechanics of their issuance in the Colonies, as had been done in England. He
pleaded that the clearest authorization of Parliament was
necessary to justify a construction in favor of general warrants and that in this case a strict interpretation of the
statutes was permissible and proper.

Had judgment been given at the conclusion of the arguments, the decision would probably have been given against
the writs, as Hutchinson himself intimated several years
later. But the chief justice persuaded the other members
of the court to suspend judgment until he ascertained *the
practice in England,* on the theory that the American customs officers were entitled to the " same authorities." In
adopting the simple expedient of finding out what the practice in England was, he was thus disregarding the whole line
of Thatcher's reasoning, the tenor of which undoubtedly was
unfamiliar and had no appeal to his practical mind.

It has been assumed by leading historians that he referred
the question to the law authorities in England.[44] If he had,
there would be room for speculation concerning the ruling
when it is recalled that Charles Pratt was then attorney
general of England. However, the channel of Hutchinson's

---

[43] *Ibid.*, p. 8.
[44] Citations *ibid.*, p. 7 include Channing, III, 5; J. T. Adams, p. 273;
Van Tyne, p. 179 n. It might be remarked that Hutchinson made no
such pretensions.

information has also been recently discovered. On March 5 he wrote to William Bollan, the agent for the province in England, who had been the prosecuting officer in the Vice-Admiralty Court in the Shirley régime, for information as to whether writs of assistance ever issued from the Exchequer except upon special information and whether they were confined to particular places and goods. Bollan replied that upon an application by the Commissioners of the Customs to the proper officer of the Court of Exchequer, general writs were made out as of course without even the affidavit or order of the court.[45] So after a second argument in November, the Superior Court gave judgment in favor of the customs officers [46] and in December granted the first of the new writs to Charles Paxton, the most unpopular man in Boston.[47] Coincidentally, as if to compensate for this decision, Charles Pratt in the same month was raised to the chief justiceship of England and thus given the opportunity several years later of stamping with the authority of law his views regarding general warrants.[48]

---

[45] Wolkins, " Bollan on Writs of Assistance," *Massachusetts Historical Society Proceedings, 1925-1926*, LIX, 414 ff.

[46] Quincy, p. 57. Gridley was this time assisted by Robert Auchmuty who soon afterwards became the new advocate general in place of Otis.

[47] *Ibid.*, pp. 418-421. See Thomas C. Haliburton, *Rule and Misrule of the English in America* (New York, 1851), p. 251, for the colonists' hatred of the customs officers.

Several writers have erred as to the results of the case. Asher L. Cornelius states that writs of assistance were declared illegal by the court. *Search and Seizure* (Indianapolis, 1926), p. 17 n. Scott says that although the writs were declared legal, none were ever issued. *Development of Constitutional Liberty in the English Colonies of America*, p. 247.

[48] During the same year, two other cases arose which also excited the indignation of the people. One was *Massachusetts Bay* v. *Paxton,* likewise prosecuted by Otis. The facts were as follows: In órder to encourage seizures for violations of the Acts of Trade, the law provided that one-third of the forfeitures should go to the province, one-third to the governor, and one-third to the officer making the seizure. An investigation, prompted by the realization that the province practically never received anything from these forfeitures, showed that the heavy expenses of these cases, such as fees to informers, lawyers, etc., were taken out of the share of the province. A suit was brought to recover these charges, upon a resolution of the legislature passed in the face of the strong opposition of Governor Bernard, but the Superior Court finally held after reversing the lower

Reference has been made to new material that has recently come to light as a result of research in the Treasury files of the Public Record Office in London. This material shows that when the question of the validity of writs of assistance was squarely put to the proper legal authorities in England, several rulings unfavorable to their validity were handed down. This interesting fact is found in a formal written opinion by the attorney general of England, William de Grey,[49] dated October 17, 1766, an opinion interesting also from the point of view of statutory construction. The occasion for this opinion had been a report of the customs officials of New London, Connecticut, that the Superior Court of that province " was at a great loss " to determine whether writs of assistance should be granted since the act of Parliament had made express provision that they should issue under the seal of the Exchequer. This, it will be noted, was the same argument which Thatcher had presented five years before. A " case " accordingly was laid before the attorney general by the Commissioners of the Customs in London, in which these questions were asked: Does the Act 7th and 8th Wm.

---

court twice that the decree of the Admiralty Court, under which the charges had been allowed, was conclusive and not open to review in an action at law. This decision was technically correct but naturally did not please the people, who claimed that they should not be exposed to writs of assistance merely to put fortunes in private pockets. Quincy, pp. 548-552.

The second and more amusing case was that of *Ewing* v. *Cradock*. The plaintiff was the owner of a ship and cargo seized for violation of the revenue laws and libelled in the Admiralty Court. With the permission of the court he agreed to pay one-half the value of the property into court in exchange for the property. He then turned around and sued the collector in trespass for the seizure. In the lower court, the jury by direction of the court brought in a verdict for the plaintiff for the full amount paid into court. The Superior Court upon appeal instructed the jury to find for the defendant, again on the ground that the decree of the Admiralty Court was conclusive. The jury disregarded these express instructions and brought in a full verdict for the plaintiff, whereupon the court, realizing it would be bad policy in view of general conditions to order a new trial, gave judgment upon the verdict but granted the defendant leave to appeal to the King in Council. The plaintiff then discreetly discharged his judgment to avoid answering on the appeal.

[49] De Grey, a distinguished lawyer, had just been promoted to the position of attorney general in August. In 1771 he was appointed chief justice of England.

III [49a] in itself empower the officers of the customs in the Plantations to enter houses and warehouses without a writ of assistance, since the writ is not mentioned in that statute in giving power to enter, etc.? If not, can such writs of assistance issue under the seal of the Court of Exchequer in England, or from any and what court in the Plantations? To which queries the following answer was made:

I think the Words of the Act will not admit of the Construction put upon them in this Case, for the Words "*and also to enter*" etc. must be connected with the preceding Words "the same Powers and Authorities" so as to run in this manner, Vizt. "*the Officers of the Revenue shall have the same Powers and Authorities as they have in England for visiting Shops etc. and also to enter Houses etc.* which words we give only a relative and not an absolute Power; and the Court of Exchequer in England do not send their Process into the Plantations, nor is there any Process in the Plantations that corresponds, with the description in the act of K. W.[50]

And a short while later, with regard to the Malcom affair in Boston, where the execution of a writ of assistance had been resisted by a merchant, the attorney general and solicitor general advised that no civil action or criminal prosecution could be brought against any of the parties who obstructed the officers inasmuch as the writ of assistance by virtue of which they entered the house and cellar was not a legal authority.[51] Particular care seems to have been taken, however, from obvious motives of prudence and expedience, that these opinions, which in effect held illegal every search and seizure ever made in the Colonies under a writ of assistance, should not reach the public ear.

To return to the course of events in Massachusetts, the

[49a] See above, page 53.

[50] *Massachusetts Historical Society Proceedings*, LVIII, 21, 71 ff. De Grey was probably considerably influenced toward this strict interpretation of the statutes by the recent holdings of the English courts that general warrants were illegal, unless sanctioned by Parliament, and by the resolution which Parliament had just adopted in April to the same effect.

[51] *Ibid.*, p. 73; Bancroft, IV, 72. In ignorance of the existence of these documents, several writers had taken the view that "from the strictly legal standpoint" Hutchinson's stand was "unassailable" and that there was little to be said on the side of the colonists. See J. T. Adams, pp. 272, 273. Compare Gray's searching inquiry into the arguments pro and con in Quincy, pp. 512-540, and his conclusion on p. 540.

unpopularity of the decision of the Superior Court was soon manifested in the actions of the legislature. With his argument in the *Writs of Assistance Case,* Otis had secured his election to the General Assembly by an overwhelming majority [52] and for ten years he was the leading spirit there in bringing on the American Revolution. On March 6, 1762, the legislature passed a bill providing for a *special* writ of assistance, to be granted by any judge or justice of the peace upon information under oath by any officer of the customs, and prohibiting all óther writs.[53] This action was similar to that taken by the legislature six years previously in the case of provincial collectors. In this connection, it seems to the writer that if the decision of the Superior Court in granting the general writs was in any way based upon the provincial statute that gave it the jurisdiction of the Court of Exchequer, and this was a very necessary (and plausible) argument in the case, then certainly the legislature had the power to take away the jurisdiction it had granted. However this may be, the attempt to abolish the general writ of assistance was unavailing, for the governor negatived it as contrary to the act of William III, after he had been careful first to inquire of those judges of the Superior Court who happened to be in town whether the two acts were inconsistent so that he could give the bill, as he wrote in a letter, "a more solemn condemnation than it deserved." [54]

---

[52] John Adams writes: "On the week of his election I happened to be at Worcester, attending the Court of Commons Pleas, of which Brigadier Ruggles was Chief Justice, when the news arrived from Boston of Mr. Otis' election. You can have no idea of the consternation among the government people. Chief Justice Ruggles . . . said, 'Out of this election will arise a damned faction, which will shake this province to its foundation.' Ruggles' foresight reached not beyond his nose. That election has shaken two continents, and will shake all four." Adams to Tudor, March 29, 1817, *Works of John Adams,* X, 248.

Hutchinson, too, showed himself a poor hand at prophecy when in 1765 he wrote of Otis: "What will posterity say of him when they reflect upon or feel the ruin he has brought upon his country." Gray, in Quincy, p. 442.

[53] See *ibid.,* pp. 495-497, for the text of the bill.

[54] *Ibid.,* p. 499. With the writer's comment above on the validity of the bill compare the form of the question asked of the judges and their answer. The question was: "Whether if this Bill should be

But the resourceful legislature had other means of showing its displeasure and had already gone to the less justifiable extremity of reducing the salaries of the Superior Court judges and of withholding the extra allowance of Hutchinson as chief justice altogether.[55]   And it went on to dismiss Bollan as agent for the province in England, without assigning any cause.   A member of the General Assembly wrote Bollan that a "number of other firebrands set the government in a flame," reduced the salaries of the judges, etc., and determined to remove him, to which end they privately insinuated to the members of the house that he favored the officers of the customs, spent his time in soliciting their affairs in England, and neglected the affairs of the government.[56]

Smuggling still went on, however, despite the fact that until after the passage of the Stamp Act in 1765 there seems to have been no trouble in executing the writs of assistance. In 1763, another order came from England for the stricter enforcement of the laws.   The effective expedient was adopted of directing the commanders of all ships on the American coast to act as officers of the customs.[57]   The following year, with the war over and money needed in England, the Grenville government decided to change the colonial system into a revenue producing system and passed the Sugar Act of 1764, which placed a less unreasonable duty on the importation of sugar and molasses.   However, the practice engendered by the impolitic and unenforced Molasses Act was too deeply entrenched, and the minds of

---

enacted, The Superior Court as a Court of Exchequer could (consistently with Such Act) grant a Writ of Assistance in pursuance of the Act of Parliament of the 7th and 8th of William the Third in the same manner as if such Bill was not enacted."   The judges replied: "That if this Bill should pass into a Law the Superior Court would be restrained from granting a Writ of Assistance in the manner they have heretofore done and in the manner such Writs of Assistance are granted by the Court of Exchequer in England." *Ibid.*, p. 497.

[55] Minot, II, 109.   See also John Marshall, *American Colonies* (Philadelphia, 1824), p. 377.

[56] *Massachusetts Historical Society Proceedings*, LIX, 421.

[57] McClellan, pp. 82 ff.; Quincy, p. 430.   See also the writ of assistance issued to Captain Bishop, *ibid.*, p. 429.

Americans, upon the introduction of this and other taxation measures, were already directed toward independence.[58]

In the Stamp Act Riot of 1765, Hutchinson's part in the *Writs of Assistance Case* was not forgotten by the rioters. Bernard wrote the following to the Lords of Trade:

> Last of all the . . . Chief Justice's house [was] destroyed with a savageness unknown in a civilized country. I mention him as Chief Justice, as it was in that character he suffered; for this connecting him with the Admiralty & Custom house was occasioned by his granting writs of assistance to the Custom house officers, upon the accession of his present Majesty; which was so strongly opposed by the Merchants that the Arguments in Court from the Bar lasted three days. The Chief Justice took the lead in the Judgement for granting Writs, and now he has paid for it.[59]

From this time on, the troubles of the customhouse officers began in earnest. The impetus given to popular feeling by the Stamp Act was hardly checked by its repeal.[60] At Newbury, a seizure of molasses was rescued by a half dozen well-manned boats which went after the officer, took the goods from him and the boat he was in, and left him to stay all night on the beach.

For a long period after the repeal of the Stamp Act, only two seizures were attempted and both were failures. After a seizure under a writ of assistance at Falmouth (now Portland) the assistance rendered by the people of the town consisted in the forcible recapture of the goods. In Boston, on September 24, 1766, the second and better known incident occurred. Two customs officials and a deputy sheriff went to the home of Captain Daniel Malcom, one of the merchants who had opposed the writs in 1761. Malcom allowed them through the house but would not permit them to enter a cer-

---

[58] McClellan, pp. 72 ff., 93.

[59] Quincy, p. 416 n.

[60] From the standpoint of expediency, what Macaulay wrote about the Stamp Act might be applied to the whole British colonial policy: "The Stamp was indefensible not because it was beyond constitutional competence of Parliament, but because it was unjust and impolitic, sterile of revenue, and fertile of discontents." Thomas B. Macaulay, *The Earl of Chatham* (1844), quoted in Hill, p. 164. Or, as Jared Ingersoll said more humorously, the whole customs system partook too much of "burning a barn to roast an Egg," a procedure naturally annoying, adds James Truslow Adams, to the owner of the barn. J. T. Adams, p. 296, citing *Ingersoll Papers*, p. 297.

tain compartment in the cellar. Arming himself with two swords and a pistol, he threatened the officers with death if they tried to break the lock. Malcom was acting most likely upon the advice of Otis, his attorney, who arrived later on. The officers went to the Governor and Council. The Council advised the Governor that its assistance was not necessary since the sheriff had the power to raise a *posse comitatus*. The officers returned in the afternoon with the unwilling high sheriff but found the house closed and surrounded by a none too friendly crowd, which offered " assistance " in such a tone that the officers saw the futility of their efforts and left the scene. Whereupon, the people were rewarded with several buckets of wine by the hardy Malcom, who had been inside with friends the whole time.[61]

This case was referred by the angry officials to England. The attorney general and solicitor general recommended that no prosecution be instituted, holding that the writ of assistance used by the customs officers was invalid.[62] And, although the Lords of the Treasury persisted, calling to the attention of the legal authorities the provincial statute giving Exchequer jurisdiction to the Superior Court and urging the continuous practice of that court in issuing the writs,[63] it may safely be assumed that these new suggestions, if not already known to the legal authorities, did not change their opinion, in view of the fact that no prosecution was later instituted and in view of the fact that it was considered necessary to legalize the writs formally in the Townshend Act of 1767.[64] Indeed, although it was probably unbeknown to both Otis and Thatcher, the fact is that they had received more satisfaction from the English authorities than from those in the province.

It did not take long to remedy the legal situation with re-

---

[61] The most complete account of this incident is the article referred to above by Wolkins, in *Massachusetts Historical Society Proceedings*, LVIII, 5-84. See also Gray, in Quincy, pp. 447-449; Channing, III, 92-93.

[62] Wolkins, in *Massachusetts Historical Society Proceedings*, LVIII, 73.

[63] *Ibid.*, pp. 73-74. See below, note 68.

[64] *Ibid.*, p. 23; Bancroft, IV, 72 n.

gard to writs of assistance. The Commissioners of the Customs in London soon communicated to the Lords of the Treasury that since the opinion of the attorney general upon this and other points was adverse, it seemed to them that the American customs officers were not vested with sufficient legal authority to carry into execution the Acts of Trade and that corrective action by Parliament was therefore necessary.[65] In March of 1767, Charles Townshend, the Chancellor of the Exchequer, was given a free hand in his colonial policy. With him on a committee to report suitable revenue bills to the House of Commons was Attorney General de Grey.[66] And the resultant statute, one of the Townshend Acts, carefully obviated the legal objections previously raised by de Grey to the validity of writs of assistance in the Colonies, by designating the superior or supreme court of each province as the court of issuance.[67] But in specifying the reason for this new provision which otherwise would be only reiterative and unnecessary, the statute used language which was sufficiently

---

[65] Commissioners of the Customs to Lords of the Treasury, October 31, 1766, in Wolkins, *Massachusetts Historical Society Proceedings*, LVIII, 65.

[66] *Ibid.*, pp. 23-24.

[67] 7 Geo. III, ch. 46, sec. 10 (1767). Gray, who was not cognizant of de Grey's first opinion, writes: " It is hard to imagine that the same House of Commons which condemned general warrants in 1766 intended to authorize general writs of assistance in 1767." Quincy, p. 534. But it should be remembered that the parliamentary resolution of 1766 expressly excepted cases provided for by act of Parliament.

John Dickinson's opinion of this section of 7 Geo. III was expressed in the ninth of his famous " Letters of a Farmer ": " I am well aware that writs of this kind may be granted at home, under the seal of the court of exchequer : but I know also, that the greatest asserters of the rights of Englishmen have always strenuously contended, that such a power was dangerous to freedom, and expressly contrary to the common law, which ever regarded a man's house as his castle, or a place of perfect security.

" If such power was in the least degree dangerous there, it must be utterly destructive to liberty here. For the people there have two securities against the undue exercise of this power by the crown, if the late act takes place. In the first place, if any injustice is done there, the person injured may bring his action against the offender, and have it tried before independent judges, who are no parties in committing the injury. Here he must be tried before dependent judges, being the men who granted the writ." The second safeguard in England emphasized by Dickinson was redress in Parliament. John Dickinson, *Political Writings* (Wilmington, 1801), I, 229-232.

ambiguous as not to call anyone's attention to the fact that the purpose was to satisfy the objections of the English law authorities themselves.[68]

That the attorney general's ruling of 1766 was deliberately kept secret is indicated also by an opinion handed down by him after the Townshend Acts, in 1768, and communicated to the American Colonies, in which he deprecated the still persistent refusal of some courts to issue any but special warrants and declared that the writs were legal in the Colonies from the time of the statute of William III which the present provision of the Townshend Act of 1767 "only meant to explain." He praised Hutchinson for his ready action in issuing the writs upon application [69] and even went so far as to maintain that the search powers of the customs officials were given by act of Parliament and not by the writ, which "does nothing more than facilitate the execution of the power by making the disobedience of the writ a contempt of court." He thus intimated that the customs officers had authority to search and seize even without the writ, another position which was inconsistent with his previous opinion.[70]

---

[68] After reciting the statute of 13 and 14 Char. II (1662) and also the statute of 7 and 8 Wm. III (1696) the act continued: "But no authority being expressly given by the said act, made in the 7th and 8th years of the reign of King William III, to any particular court to grant such writs of assistance for the officers of the customs in the said plantations, it is doubted whether such officers can legally enter houses and other places on land, to search for and seize goods in the manner directed by the said recited acts: To obviate which doubts for the future, and in order to carry the intention of the said recited acts into effectual execution, be it enacted. . . ."

Incidentally, the act of 1662 was so worded as to permit the issuance of a writ to any "person or persons," whereas in the Townshend Act this was limited to customs officers. In 1761 in the *Writs of Assistance Case*, Otis had raised the point that the act of 1662 was so broadly drawn that the writs were not even restricted to customs officers but could be issued to anybody at all.

[69] He did not mention and thus placed no reliance upon the provincial statute giving exchequer jurisdiction to the Superior Court, declaring that from the general import of 7 and 8 Wm. III (1696), the writs "ought to have been set on foot from that time in America."

[70] Cf. note 20, above. The text of the opinion may be found in Quincy, pp. 452-454. It is true that the opinion was based primarily on the Townshend Act, but an obvious exception must be taken to the statement by Wolkins that the ruling "rested solidly on that particular Townshend Act of 1767, and was in no particular inconsistent

The Townshend Acts, by the legalization of writs of assistance, aided little in the administration of the law. This was
true both in New England, where the people resisted, and in
most of the other colonies, where the courts themselves were
obdurate. In 1768, a riot resulted when John Hancock's
sloop " Liberty " was seized under a writ for landing Madeira
wines without payment of duties and was taken out and
anchored under the guns of a man-of-war in the harbor.[71]
In 1769, the same year that the Commissioners of the Customs in America sent out instructions to their subordinates
insisting upon the use of writs of assistance,[72] Hutchinson
wrote that he doubted whether any customhouse officer would
venture to make a seizure.[73]

The last pertinent incident to occur in Massachusetts took
place in 1772. At a meeting of the inhabitants of Boston, a
committee of twenty-one was appointed " to state the Rights
of the Colonists . . . to communicate and publish these in the
several towns in this province, and to the World, as the sense
of the town." [74] Otis was a member of the committee and
the presentation of its report was his last public act. One of
the " Infringements and Violations of Rights " drawn up by
the committee consisted of a lengthy article decrying the general search powers of customs officers, much like Otis' argument in the *Writs of Assistance Case* of 1761.[75] It was

---

with his opinion of October 17, 1766." *Massachusetts Historical
Society Proceedings*, LVIII, 23.

[71] The crowd was not only irked by the violence of the captors but
also thought that the seizure, which was made near sunset, was
illegal, due to an erroneous impression that the restriction in the writ
to daytime search of buildings applied to vessels as well. Quincy,
pp. 456-464; Channing, pp. 94-95. Compare Hunt, X, 88-89. Upon
being adjudged forfeit in the Admiralty Court, the ship was bought
by the Collector of Boston and used as a coast guard. Her existence
in that capacity was short-lived. In 1769, a Newport mob, provoked
by her seizures of vessels on unfounded suspicions and by the crew's
insolence, scuttled and burned the ship.

[72] Samuel E. Morison, *Sources and Documents Illustrating the
American Revolution, 1764-1788* (Oxford, 1923), p. 74.

[73] Governor Bernard stated: " That there has been no rescue late is
very True; & the reason is that there has been no seizure." Quincy,
p. 463.

[74] *Boston Town Records, 1770-1777* (Boston, 1887), p. 93. See also
Charles Borgeaud, *Adoption and Amendment of Constitutions* (New
York, 1895), p. 15.

[75] *Boston Town Records*, pp. 100-101.

singularly fitting that the career of this patriot should close as it had begun with a denunciation of the general warrant.

Most of the other colonial courts, as stated, refused to grant general writs of assistance even after the Townshend Act had set at rest all technical objections to their legality.[76] The concept of "constitutionality" was already gaining ground in the Colonies and besides, the spirit of defiance and revolution was already in the air. In Connecticut, before the Townshend Act of 1767, the judges of the Superior Court had raised the correct legal question, namely, that under existing law the writ could issue only from the English Court of Exchequer, a position which had been the occasion for and had been acceded to by de Grey's first opinion. The customs officers applied again for the writs in March, 1768, relying this time on the Townshend Act, but this time they were refused on the ground of "unconstitutionality." Two months later an unsuccessful attempt was made in the legislature to remove Chief Justice Trumbull for this action. Another application was made the following year, supported by de Grey's second opinion. The court referred the request to the consideration of the General Assembly. A committee appointed for that purpose declined, as such, to render an opinion for the reason that the question was properly one for the court. As individuals, however, and not as members of the legislature, they advised the court not to grant the warrants. There is no record of the action taken by the Superior Court. But the statement by Trumbull as late as 1770 that he believed that all the Colonies, with the exception of Massachusetts and New Hampshire, were united with Connecticut on the question of writs of assistance, seems to put all inference to rest with regard to the decision in Connecticut.[77]

---

[76] See generally, Gray, in Quincy, pp. 500-511.

[77] Trumbull to Johnson, January 29, 1770, *Massachusetts Historical Society Collections* (5th Ser.), IX, 402; also *ibid.*, pp. 292, 374-375.

Johnson, the agent for Connecticut in England, wrote to Roger Sherman, one of the judges of the Superior Court of Connecticut and a person whose opinions are important because of his connection with events which will be discussed in the following chapter: " You justly object that the officer might as well be authorized by his commission as by such a writ, and the attendance of the civil officer is only to

New Hampshire is the only other colony besides Massachusetts known to have granted general writs before 1767. After that date, of course, they continued to be issued in that colony. The records of Rhode Island, where the defiance of trade laws and customs officers was notorious, contain no evidence that writs of assistance were granted there. It is very questionable that action in favor of the writs was ever taken, especially in view of the statement of its chief justice in 1769 when the question was before the Supreme Court of the colony, that he agreed with Trumbull "that Union Sentiment & Practice of the Court of Each Colony is needful on this Occasion." [78] In New York, several writs were issued in 1768, but their form is unknown. Here too, in view of Trumbull's assertion referred to above, they might have been special, as in Virginia. It is known that in New Jersey the chief justice was "laboring under difficulties" with regard to writs of assistance even after 1767 and the inference is further strengthened by the absence of any trace of the writs in the New Jersey records.

The second opinion of de Grey specifically criticized the refusal of Chief Justice Allen of Pennsylvania to issue general writs of assistance. From the fact that in 1769 a customs officer attempting to force an entrance to a building had no writ of assistance in his possession at the time but went to get one from the chief justice when resistance was offered,[79] it would appear probable that the latter did not change his position and granted only special writs even after the censure of Attorney General de Grey. The Maryland records of this period reveal no material.[80] In Virginia,

---

preserve the peace, which the Revenue officer has not the authority to command, sho'd any disturbance happen. The intention of this provision is therefore, plainly to bring the common law in aid of the Revenue Laws, and to give the latter, all that countenance and sanction, which may be derived from the former." Johnson to Sherman, September 28, 1768, as quoted by Gray, in Quincy, pp. 502-503 n.

[78] *Ibid.*, p. 507 n.

[79] Sheppard to Board of Commissioners, April, 1769, *Massachusetts Historical Society Collections* (4th Ser., 1871), X, 612. Channing seems to assume in his reference to this case that the writ of assistance used was of the ordinary type, that is, a general writ. III, 95 n.

[80] See above, note 20.

the application of the attorney general of the province for general warrants, relying on de Grey's second opinion, was strenuously opposed by the Virginia bar which insisted that the model writ sent over from England was by no means conformable to the act of Parliament and was too general. The Supreme Court of Justice acceded to this view and granted only special writs.

As for South Carolina, general writs of assistance did issue there at some later date, according to a statement by Judge William Henry Drayton of that province. This appears in a letter which he wrote on August 10, 1774, to the First Continental Congress which was then soon to meet, urging that body to address an " American Claim of Rights " to the king. South Carolina, he wrote, formerly had an independent bench of judges to which the attorney general had applied in vain for writs of assistance, described by Drayton as " of a more pernicious nature than general warrants." [81] However, upon the subsequent appointment of a bench more favorable to the Crown, he continued, the writs were unhesitatingly granted " without an investigation of the merits." [82] It may be stated at this point that the petition which the Continental Congress later addressed to the king on October 26, 1774, contained the following clause as one of the colonists' grievances: " The officers of the customs are empowered to break open and enter houses, without the authority of any civil magistrate, founded on legal information." And finally in Georgia, Chief Justice Anthony Stokes

---

[81] The 5th article of the list of abuses pointed out by Drayton, writing under the name of " Freeman," was as follows: " By Judges now-a-days granting to the Customs to lie dormant in their possession, writs of assistance in the nature of general warrants, by which, without any crime charged and without any suspicion, a petty officer has power to cause the doors and locks of any man to be broke open, to enter his most private cabinet, and thence to take and carry away whatever he shall in his pleasure deem uncustomed goods." Article 6 of his " Claim of Rights " declared: " That no writs of assistance ought to be issued to the Customs, but in the nature of writs or warrants to search for goods stolen—general writs or warrants being illegal." *Ibid.*, pp. 15 ff. On account of the writing of this letter he was superseded as King's Judge and suspended as one of the Privy Councillors. *Ibid.*, pp. 39 ff.

[82] Robert W. Gibbes, *Documentary History of the American Revolution, 1764-1776* (New York, 1855), I, 21.

was outvoted by the three associate judges and general writs were refused.[83]

But it was not very long before the sincerity of the colonists with respect to general warrants was put to the test and found incapable of standing the strain of extreme circumstances. On August 28, 1777, Congress, then in session in Philadelphia, received information that a large British army had landed at the head of the Chesapeake. It thereupon recommended to the Supreme Executive Council of Pennsylvania the arrest of certain persons, most of them Quakers, who had shown a disposition inimical to the American cause, "together with all such papers in their possession as may be of a political nature." Congress also recommended the seizure of the records and papers of the Meeting of Sufferings, an institution of the Quakers.[84]

These persons were arrested together with a number of others, many of them citizens of wealth and influence. There was neither trial nor hearing. They were hurried to confinement, their houses were searched, and desks were broken open in a general fishing expedition for compromising papers. Twenty-three of these people who were being detained at Mason's Lodge prepared a remonstrance to the President and Council of Pennsylvania. This interesting document[85] set forth the ninth and tenth sections of the Pennsylvania Declaration of Rights adopted just the year before, the ninth guaranteeing the essentials of a fair trial, and the tenth prohibiting general warrants.[86] It went on to declare that the warrant issued by the Council had authorized the messengers to search all papers on the bare possibility that something political might be found, but without the least ground for a suspicion of the kind. It stated that the warrant required papers relative to the Meeting of Sufferings to be seized, without limiting the search to any house or houses, under color of which every house in the city could have been

---

[83] Channing, III, 5 n.

[84] *Journals of Congress, 1774-1788*, II, 246, 251.

[85] See Niles, *Principles and Acts of the Revolution*, pp. 255-256.

[86] See pages 80-81, below, for a discussion of the search and seizure provision of the Pennsylvania Declaration of Rights.

invaded; that the messengers had refused to give copies of
the process to those they arrested and in the absence of some,
had broken open desks and other private repositories and had
carried off domestic papers, printed books, and other material
not within the terms of the warrant; [87] that the warrant
limited no time for the duration of imprisonment, nor pointed
to any hearing, which was an absolute requirement in a
legal warrant. The remonstrants protested this general warrant and called upon the officials addressed to reconcile their
conduct with their repeated declarations in favor of general
liberty.

Congress recommended that the Council hear the peti-
tioners. The Council replied that it did not have the time
to undertake what might consume a great deal of time, " in
the midst of the present load of important business . . . of
which that of embodying the militia is not the least part,"
and that as great injury might result to the Commonwealth
if any further time were spent in the matter, it earnestly
requested that Congress should grant the hearing. Whereupon Congress, also under the stress of the impending
invasion, resolved that it would be improper to enter into
any hearing of the remonstrants, since they were inhabitants
of Pennsylvania.[88]

The whole record bespeaks half-hearted action and the
feeling of shameful necessity. The prisoners were ordered
sent to Virginia, notwithstanding the issuance of a writ of
habeas corpus by Chief Justice McKean, which the state
authorities disregarded.[89] The whole proceeding may better

---

[87] The papers were turned over to Congress and some of them were
ordered published. *Journals of Congress*, II, 251, 256. Later on, the
Meeting of Sufferings was able to recover all the papers taken from it.
Isaac Sharpless, *A History of Quaker Government in Pennsylvania*
(Philadelphia, 1900), II, 164-165.

[88] *Journals of Congress*, II, 256, 257.

[89] Sharpless, II, 159. These men are known to history as the
" Virginia Exiles." They were finally returned to their homes in
April, 1778, through the efforts and influence of Washington.
See *ibid.*, chap. vii, for the best account of the incident. See also,
George O. Trevelyan, *The American Revolution* (London, 1907), III,
271-273; Lorenzo Sabine, *Tories of the American Revolution* (Boston,
1864), *passim.*

be described as extra-legal rather than illegal, justified in the
opinion of Congress and the Council on the ground of military
necessity.[90]   It is exceedingly doubtful that such an occur-
rence would have taken place in more normal times.   But it
brings to mind what James Madison said twelve years later,
that wherever there is an interest and power to do wrong,
wrong will generally be done, and not less readily by a
powerful and interested majority in a democracy than by
a powerful and interested prince in a monarchy.[91]

---

[90] Sharpless, II, 159.   Compare the holding of the United States
Supreme Court in *Ex parte Milligan*, 4 Wall. 2, 18 L. ed. 281 (1866).
But cf. *Luther* v. *Borden*, 7 How. 1, 12 L. ed. 581 (1849).

[91] Madison to Jefferson, October 17, 1788, in *Writings of James
Madison* (Gaillard Hunt, ed., New York, 1904), V, 272 ff.   " Experience proves the inefficacy of a bill of rights on those occasions when
its control is most needed.   Repeated violations of these parchment
barriers have been committed by overbearing majorities in every
State. . . .   Wherever the real power in a Government lies, there is
the danger of oppression."   See this letter and Jefferson's reply for
a most interesting and penetrating discussion of the place and function of a bill of rights.   *Writings of Thomas Jefferson* (Library ed.,
Washington, 1903), V, 309 ff.

CHAPTER III

THE FOURTH AMENDMENT

The first American precedent of a constitutional character for the Fourth Amendment was the famous Virginia Bill of Rights of 1776.[1] This Bill of Rights was drawn up almost entirely by George Mason.[2] But although few changes were made in Mason's original propositions and only two additional articles inserted by the convention which adopted the Bill of Rights, we find upon closer examination that the prohibition of general warrants was one of these additions. The clause was agreed to in committee and Mason was not its author.[3]

As a matter of fact, Mason's opinion concerning these additions and alterations was rather unfavorable. In a note appended to his own first draft of the propositions which he submitted, in which there was no mention of search and seizure or general warrants, he described the additions made by the convention as not of a fundamental nature, and added: " This Declaration of Rights was the first in America;[4] it received few alterations or additions in the Virginia Convention (some of them not for the better) and was afterwards closely imitated by the other United States." [5]

[1] Adopted by the Williamsburg Convention, June 12, 1776. For text, see Hill, *Liberty Documents*, pp. 166 ff.; Benjamin P. Poore, *Federal and State Constitutions*, (Washington, 1877), II, 1909. See also page 33 n., above.

[2] The declaration was drafted by Mason and was changed only slightly in one particular by James Madison. Hill, p. 166. See also Kate M. Rowland, *Life of George Mason* (New York, 1892), I, chap. vii; *ibid.*, pp. 433–441; Niles, *Principles and Acts of the Revolution*, pp. 121 ff.

[3] To facilitate comparison, the various state search and seizure provisions will be set out at large wherever any difference is noted. The Virginia clause reads as follows: " X. That general warrants whereby an officer or messenger may be commanded to search suspected places without evidence of a fact committed, or to seize any person or persons not named, or whose offense is not particularly described and supported by evidence, are grievous and oppressive and ought not to be granted." Poore, II, 1909.

[4] " The enlightened part of Europe have given us the greatest credit for inventing the instrument of security for the rights of the people." *Writings of Thomas Jefferson*, VII, 301.

[5] Rowland, I, 436; Mason to Mercer, October 2, 1778, *ibid.*, p. 237; facsimile of the document at p. 240, *ibid.* Although it is clear that

79

However, the very fact that the provision was inserted by the convention, considering that the proposals which Mason submitted met with such favor otherwise and were adopted so completely, indicates the importance with which it was regarded by others on the committee and in the convention. Moreover, the opinions of such members as Patrick Henry, Edmund Randolph, and James Madison may be gleaned from the views which they expressed upon other occasions.

Several writers have cited the Declaration of Independence as a precedent for the Fourth Amendment.[6] An inspection of that historic document, however, fails to disclose any direct reference to general warrants, writs of assistance, or the principle of freedom from unreasonable search.[7] This omission is somewhat surprising when several facts are taken into consideration. The main part of the Declaration was given over to a statement of grievances against the system of British rule in the Colonies. Samuel Adams and John Adams were signers. And John Adams not only was a member of the drafting committee but was the one who revised the Declaration after it had left the pen of Jefferson.[8] A clear opportunity was there lost to point to a practice in the Colonies which could be denounced upon the then recent authority of the English courts themselves.

After the Virginia Bill of Rights, however, some provision with regard to search and seizure was assured a place in every state declaration or bill of rights.[9] On September 28, 1776,

---

Mason did not regard the tenth article as fundamental, it would not seem that he directed his subsequent remark against it or that he had any objection to it. The wording of his propositions was unnecessarily changed in a number of places, and it is more likely that it was about these changes that he wrote " some of them not for the better."

[6] Francis N. Thorpe, *Constitutional History of the United States* (Chicago, 1901), II, 207; Frederic J. Stimson, *Law of the Federal and State Constitutions of the United States* (Boston, 1908), p. 149, n. 10.

[7] The text of the Declaration is in Hill, p. 183; Carl N. Becker, *Declaration of Independence* (New York, 1922), pp. 5 ff. The grievance possibly was meant to be comprehended in this one among those noted against George III: " He has . . . sent hither swarms of Officers to harass our people. . . ."

[8] Lecky, *England in the Eighteenth Century*, III, 491-499.

[9] The New Jersey Constitution (July 3, 1776) contained no formal

the state of Pennsylvania adopted its Declaration of Rights. Section 10 was the first precedent which closely approximated what is now the Fourth Amendment to the United States Constitution. It contained all the elements of the Fourth Amendment, in that it was not merely a condemnation of general warrants like the Virginia clause but also stated the broader principle, that is, freedom from unreasonable search and seizure.[10] In addition, it made oath or affirmation essential to the validity of the warrant.[11]

Article 23 of the Maryland Declaration of Rights, which was adopted November 11, 1776, was patterned after neither the Pennsylvania nor the Virginia model. Although it did not state the general principle, as did the former, it did require, unlike the latter, the essential of oath or affirmation.[12] On the contrary, Virginia's other neighboring state, North Carolina, in the Declaration of Rights which it adopted December 18, 1776, took the phraseology of Virginia's Article

---

bill of rights, although there were several provisions properly referable thereto, e. g., protection of rights of accused and freedom of religious worship. There is no mention of search and seizure.

[10] The wording of this and similar provisions of other early constitutions seems to show that the general principle was stated merely as a basis for the minor premise condemning general warrants and that the abuse attempted to be prevented was that of general warrants only.

[11] " X. That the people have a right to hold themselves, their houses, papers, and possessions free from search and seizure, and therefore warrants without oaths or affirmation first made, affording a sufficient foundation for them, and whereby any officer or messenger may be commanded or required to search suspected places, or to seize any person or persons, his or their property, are contrary to that right, and ought not to be granted." Poore, II, 1542. By freedom " from search and seizure " is obviously not meant all search and seizure, as the next clause attests. The word " unreasonable " is imputed.

[12] The Maryland clause reads: " That all warrants, without oath or affirmation, to search suspected places, or to seize any person or property, are grievous and oppressive; and all general warrants—to search suspected places, or to apprehend suspected persons without naming or describing the place, or the person in special—are illegal, and ought not to be granted." Poore, I, 819. What exactly is meant by declaring unverified warrants to be *grievous and oppressive* and general warrants *illegal*, is not clear, but it is doubtful whether any legal distinction was intended. It may be observed that in the recommendations for amendment of the Federal Constitution made by a committee of the Maryland Convention that ratified the Constitution, the word " dangerous " was substituted for " illegal."

10 almost verbatim.[13]   The Constitution of Vermont (July 8, 1777), on the other hand, copied Section 10 of the Pennsylvania Declaration.[14]

Massachusetts was next in line with Article 14 of the Declaration of Rights of 1780.[15] Its more elaborate wording was not taken from any of the other constitutions and offered the first expression of the phrase " unreasonable searches and seizures " which ultimately found its way into the Fourth Amendment. Finally, in the New Hampshire Bill of Rights of 1784, the Massachusetts article was duplicated.[16] Accordingly, seven different states had constitutional provisions which were to serve as precedents for the Fourth Amendment.[17]

---

[13] " XI. That general warrants—whereby an officer or messenger may be commanded to search suspected places, without evidence of the fact committed, or to seize any person or persons, not named, whose offenses are not particularly described and supported by evidence—are dangerous to liberty, and ought not to be granted." Poore, II, 1409.

[14] *Ibid.*, p. 1860; repeated in section 12 of the Declaration of 1786, *ibid.*, p. 1868. Vermont was not one of the original thirteen states. Its territory was claimed by the surrounding states of New York, New Hampshire, and Massachusetts. At the beginning of the Revolution, the people of Vermont sought independence, accordingly, not only from Great Britain but from these states as well.

[15] " Art. XIV. Every subject has a right to be secure from all unreasonable searches and seizures of his person, his house, his papers, and all his possessions. All warrants, therefore, are contrary to this right, if the cause or foundation of them be not previously supported by oath or affirmation, and if the order in the warrant to a civil officer, to make search in suspected places, or to arrest one or more suspected persons, or to seize their property, be not accompanied with a special designation of the person or objects of search, arrest, or seizure; and no warrant ought to be issued, but in cases, and with the formalities prescribed by the laws." Poore, I, 959.

[16] New Hampshire Bill of Rights, section 19. Poore, II, 1282.

[17] Virginia, Pennsylvania, Maryland, North Carolina, Vermont (in two instances), Massachusetts, and New Hampshire. The Connecticut Constitution of 1776 provided: " No man's person shall be arrested—no man's goods shall be taken away from him, unless clearly warranted by the laws of this state." Poore, I, 258. The only case listed in the *Century Digest* involving search and seizure and an illegal search warrant before 1789 was one in Connecticut. In 1787, it was there held that a warrant was illegal which authorized a search for stolen property in all places where the complainant might suspect such property would be found and also the arrest of any persons with whom the goods should be found or any persons suspected of the theft. *Frisbie v. Butler*, Kirby 213. The constitutions of the other of the original thirteen states either had no formal bill of rights or stated only a few of those rights.

Nevertheless, a study of the forces and influences which led to the adoption of the Fourth Amendment cannot be conveniently isolated. The Amendment was carried into the Constitution in response to a wide clamor for a bill of rights, as one of the more important rights contained in such instruments. The introduction of the provision into the Federal Constitution must consequently be traced in the demand that a bill of rights should be included.

In 1787, the Constitutional Convention, composed of many of the most eminent and able men in America, met in Philadelphia to revise the unsatisfactory Articles of Confederation.[18] After several months' deliberation this Convention brought forward that document which Gladstone, in an oft-repeated statement, eulogized as " the most wonderful work ever struck off at a given time by the brain and purpose of man." [19] Yet this new constitution succeeded of adoption only by the narrowest of margins. The labors of the framers had resulted not merely in revision of the old Articles but in the establishment of an entirely new system, with a strong central government exercising extensive powers and acting upon the people directly. One of the foremost popular objections to the Constitution, therefore,—a defect which afforded its opponents a splendid opportunity to seize upon the fears. and prejudices of the populace—was the omission of a declaration of rights. The question arises then: Why was such a declaration not inserted by the framers in the original Constitution?

According to available records of the proceedings of the Convention, the question of a bill of rights did not arise until five days before adjournment and then, apparently, only as an incidental matter. On September 12, 1787, Mr. Williamson observed that no provision had yet been made for juries in civil cases. The reply was made by Mr. Gorham that it was not possible successfully to distinguish between

---

[18] See the resolution of Congress calling the convention in *Debates on the Federal Constitution* (Jonathan Elliot, ed., Washington, 1836), I, 120.

[19] W. E. Gladstone, *Gleanings of Past Years* (London, 1879), I, 211-212.

equity cases and cases where juries were proper and that Congress could safely be trusted in the premises, whereupon Mr. Gerry also urged a clause to secure the right of trial by jury. It was at that moment, according to Madison's notes, that the thought of a bill of rights occurred to Colonel Mason.

Col. Mason perceived the difficulty mentioned by Mr. Gorham. The jury cases cannot be specified. A general principle laid down on this and some other points would be sufficient. He wished the plan had been prefaced with a Bill of Rights, and would second a motion if made for that purpose. It would give great quiet to the people; and with the aid of the State declarations, a bill might be prepared in a few hours.

Mr. Gerry concurred in the idea and moved for a Committee to prepare a Bill of Rights. Col. Mason 2ded the motion.[20]

Mr. Sherman was for securing the rights of the people where requisite. The State Declarations of Rights are not repealed by the Constitution; and being in force are sufficient. There are many cases where juries are proper which cannot be discriminated. The Legislature may be safely trusted.

Col. Mason. The laws of the U. S. are to be paramount to State Bills of Rights. On the question of a Com. to prepare a Bill of Rights.

N. H. No. Mas. Abst. Ct. No. N. J. No. Pa. No. Del. No. Md. No. Va. No. N. C. No. S. C. No. Geo. No. (Ayes—0; Noes—10; Absent—1).[21]

---

[20] Note that Gerry and Mason were two of the three men who refused to sign the Constitution at the close of the Convention. Luther Martin of Maryland, one of the most bitter opponents of the Constitution, wrote in the Maryland Journal (March 21, 1788) that he had drawn up a motion a few days before he left the Convention (September 4, 1787) to have a committee appointed to prepare a bill of rights, and would have presented it but for the assurance of several members that the motion would be in vain. Max Farrand, *Records of the Federal Convention* (New Haven, 1911), III, 290-291; *The Federalist and Other Constitutional Papers* (E. H. Scott, ed., Chicago, 1894), II, 689-690.

[21] Farrand, II, 587-588. This is the vote as recorded in Madison's manuscript. However, in the *Papers of James Madison* (H. D. Gilpin, ed., Washington, 1840), III, 1566, the motion is reported to have been lost not unanimously, but on a 5-5 geographical division, as follows: " New Hampshire, Connecticut, New Jersey, Pennsylvania, Delaware, aye—5; Maryland, Virginia, North Carolina, South Carolina, Georgia, no—5; Massachusetts, absent." This found its way into later editions of Madison's notes, such as *Journal of the Federal Convention kept by James Madison* (E. H. Scott, ed., Chicago, 1894), p. 717 and in Elliot's *Debates*, V, 538, the supplementary volume by Elliot giving Madison's minutes. Madison had had his notes copied " under his own eye " by his brother-in-law, John C. Pagne. *Debates in the Federal Convention of 1787* (G. Hunt and J. B. Scott, edd., New York, 1920), p. xxii. It was in this transcript that the 5-5 vote first appeared, from which it went into the editions

Two days later, Mr. Pinckney and Mr. Gerry moved to insert a declaration that the liberty of the press should be inviolably observed. Mr. Sherman argued: " It is unnecessary. The power of Congress does not extend to the Press." The motion was defeated, this time, however, by the much closer vote of 6-5. New Hampshire, Massachusetts, Maryland, Virginia, and South Carolina voted in favor of the motion.[22]

This argument by Sherman of the conclusiveness of the delegated powers theory upon the question of the protection of civil rights, taken in connection with his previous statement that the state bills of rights were sufficient safeguards, is the only recorded statement of any member of the Convention which might explain the failure of the Convention to insert a bill of rights in the original Constitution.[23]   But the absence

---

mentioned above. The manuscript of the official Journal of the Convention merely states that the motion " passed in the negative " (*Documentary History of the Constitution* (Washington, 1894), I, 194), but the record of votes turned over to the secretary of state by Washington in 1796 again gave the vote as 10-0 against the motion. *Ibid.*, p. 241; Farrand, II, 583. Since the vote as recorded by the secretary of the Convention agrees with Madison's original manuscript, the error seems to have been on the part of the copyist. See George Bancroft, *History of the Formation of the Constitution* (New York, 1882), II, 210, n. 1; Hunt and Scott, *Debates*, p. 557, n. 1. The error went over into such leading works as George T. Curtis, *Constitutional History of the United States* (New York, 1903), I, 644, and Rowland, II, 172. For a general discussion of the history of Madison's records, see the introductions in Farrand, and Hunt and Scott.

[22] Farrand, II, 611, 618, 620. Madison makes the count 7-4 by listing New Hampshire in the negative, but this would seem to be a mistake, in view of the fact that the vote is recorded as 6-5 in both the Journal and the notes of McHenry of Maryland.

[23] The framers clearly did not realize the potentialities and possibilities of the system which they were formulating, especially of the " necessary and proper " clause. See in this connection the letter from Washington to Lafayette, below, n. 47. As stated by Charles Warren: " They failed to see that while possibly there were no specific powers vested in Congress to infringe the freedom of speech or of the press, or to impose unreasonable search and seizure without search warrant, legislation which would so operate might be enacted in the necessary and proper execution of one of the specific powers. For instance, in the collection of taxes, Congress (unless restrained by a Bill of Rights) might order an unreasonable seizure without search warrant as a necessary and proper means of executing the taxing power." Charles Warren, *The Making of the Constitution* (Boston, 1929), p. 509. See also, *ibid.*, p. 769; John A. Jameson, *The Constitutional Convention* (Chicago, 1887), pp. 90 ff. The limited view taken of the powers of Congress by many of the pro-

of mature deliberation or extended discussion and the summary disposition of the problem, which was thus presented for
the first time only a few days before adjournment,[24] confirm
the conclusion that the framers failed to realize its importance and to accord it merited consideration. Thus James
Wilson, a leading member of the Convention, no more than a
month and a half later in response to a request in the Pennsylvania Convention that he "communicate some of the
reasons (and undoubtedly they must have been powerful
ones) which induced the late federal convention to omit a
bill of rights,"[25] was forced to reply:

> The truth is, Sir, that this circumstance, which has since occasioned
> so much clamor and debate, never struck the mind of any member in
> the late convention till, I believe, within three days of the dissolution
> of that body, and even then of so little account was the idea that it
> passed off in a short conversation, without introducing a formal
> debate or assuming the shape of a motion.[26]

It is of course true that the framers had worked during
a hot summer, that the end was actually in sight, and that
they were in a hurry to get through.[27] By this inadvert-
ence,[28] however, they placed in the hands of the opponents

---

ponents of the Constitution is illustrated in the statement of George
Nicholas in the Virginia Convention, with regard to the necessity of
a bill of rights, that outside of treason, Congress could only define
and punish piracies and felonies committed on the high seas and
offenses against the law of nations; that to define or prescribe the
punishment of any other crime whatever would be a violation of the
Constitution. Elliot's *Debates*, III, 451, 466.

[24] Although Mason and Gerry later made much of the omission, it
would seem that the matter was more of an afterthought with them
than anything else, from the fact that they had not brought it more
prominently before the Convention and at a more propitious time.

[25] J. B. McMaster and F. D. Stone, *Pennsylvania and the Federal
Constitution* (Philadelphia, 1888), p. 251.

[26] *Ibid.*, p. 253. So little impression did the discussion make on
Wilson that he forgot that a motion had been made. He repeated
this error in a later speech and then went on to say: ". . . Certainly,
before we heard this so violently supported out of doors, some pains
ought to have been taken to have its fate tried within." He concluded, however, that a bill of rights was unnecessary and improper.
See also, Elliot's *Debates*, II, 435, 453.

[27] Farrand, *The Framing of the Constitution* (New Haven, 1913),
p. 185.

[28] Washington wrote to Lafayette: "There was not a member of
the Convention, I believe, who had the least objection to what is contended for by the advocates of a Bill of Rights. . . ." *Writings of
George Washington* (W. C. Ford, ed., New York, 1891), XI, 256.

of the Constitution a powerful and effective weapon which played an important rôle in the ensuing struggle for ratification.[29] "I believe," said Madison in the first Congress, "the great mass of the people who opposed it disliked it because it did not contain effectual provisions against the encroachment on particular rights and those safeguards which they have been long accustomed to have interposed between them and the magistrate who exercises the sovereign power."[30]

The Convention adjourned on the 17th of September. The Constitution was presented to Congress on the 20th. Led by such able men as Richard Henry Lee of Virginia, Nathan Dane of Massachusetts, and Melanchton Smith of New York (all of them had been on the committee which only two months before had reported the liberal Northwest Ordinance[31]), a considerable opposition in that body was already organized. An attempt was made by Lee to append a bill of rights and several other amendments before submitting the Constitution to the states.[32] He contended that it was the undoubted right and duty of Congress to insert amendments where the essential safeguards of liberty had been omitted[33] but his proposal was finally defeated by the

---

[29] "It is much easier to alarm people than to inform them," wrote a supporter of the Constitution. Davie to Iredell, quoted in Warren, p. 762.

Concerning the motion for a bill of rights made during the Convention, Bancroft writes: "The declaration of American independence, by the truths which it announced, called forth sympathy in all parts of the world. Could the Constitution of the United States have been accompanied by a like declaration of the principles on which it rested, the States would have been held together by the holiest and strongest bonds" (II, 209-210).

[30] *Annals of Cong.*, 1st Cong., 1st sess., p. 450. In this connection, see especially George T. Curtis, *History of the Constitution of the United States* (New York, 1860), II, 497-498.

[31] Thorpe, II, 1 ff.

[32] The declaration proposed by Lee contained the following clause: "That the Citizens shall not be exposed to unreasonable searches, seizure of their persons, houses, papers, or property." J. C. Ballagh, *Letters of Richard Henry Lee* (New York, 1914), II, 442. Note that he proposed only an expression of the general principle. Madison writes: "He [Lee] proposed a bill of Rights,—provision for juries in civil cases, & several other things corresponding with the ideas of Colonel M[ason.]" Madison to Washington, September 30, 1787, in *Writings of Madison*, V, 5-6.

[33] *Ibid.*

advocates of the Constitution on the argument that it would be inexpedient to have amendments made by Congress.[34] Lee's party, however, did succeed to this extent: They had Congress transmit the Constitution without any expression of approval.[35]

The omission of a bill of rights was soon an active subject of discussion in newspapers,[36] pamphlets,[37] correspondence, and conventions. George Mason, who had refused to sign the Constitution, gave first place to this in his list of objections.[38] Elbridge Gerry of Massachusetts, another of the

---

[34] Curtis, *History of the Constitution*, II, 500.

[35] Lee to Mason, October 1, 1787, in Ballagh, II, 439; Gaillard Hunt, *Life of James Madison* (New York, 1902), p. 168. For an account of the proceedings in Congress, see also Bancroft, II, 226 ff.

[36] Thorpe, II, 7. Numerous essays which appeared in newspapers are collected in Paul L. Ford, *Essays on the Constitution* (Brooklyn, 1892), and selections appear also in *The Federalist and Other Constitutional Papers*. For arguments favorable to the Constitution as it stood originally, see in the last mentioned reference, pp. 490, 612, 667-668; and for the other side of the question, pp. 538 ff., 551-552, 555 ff., and 688 ff.

A typical Anti-Federalist attack is illustrated in the following widely circulated newspaper letter: " Among the blessings of the new proposed Government our correspondent enumerated: 1. The Liberty of the Press abolished. . . . 5. Fivefold taxes. 6. No trial by jury in civil cases. 7. General Search Warrants. 8. Excise laws, custom house officers. . . ." *Independent Gazetteers* (Philadelphia, October 6, 1787), quoted in Warren, p. 763.

[37] For the writings of the numerous pamphleteers of the time, see the selections in Ford, pp. 723, 754, 773 ff., 849-851, 871-873, 885-886, 906 ff.

Richard Henry Lee in his " Letters of a Federal Farmer," after stating that the establishment of some private rights by the Constitution, such as prohibition of bills of attainder and *ex post facto* laws, implied the necessity of establishing others, went on to say: " There are other essential rights, which we have justly understood to be the rights of freemen; as freedom from hasty and unreasonable search warrants, warrants not founded on oath, and not issued with due caution, for searching and seizing men's papers, property and persons." Ford, *Pamphlets on the Constitution* (Brooklyn, 1888), p. 315. Warren writes (p. 767) that this pamphlet, which contained an able and restrained exposition of the Anti-Federalist arguments, had a much more widespread circulation and a much greater influence than the *Federalist*, the influence of which has been generally overstated. Lee's pamphlet was very popular and went to four editions and several thousand copies. Ford, *Pamphlets*, p. 277. See also Bancroft, II, 230.

[38] Farrand, *Records*, II, 637. Mason gave copies of his " Objections," which he had written on the reverse side of his copy of the Constitution, to several persons. It was later published in pamphlet form.

three who had refused to sign,[39] emphasized the omission as one of his principal reasons for not signing.[40] Robert Yates of New York and Luther Martin of Maryland, who withdrew from the Convention before its close and became leaders of the opposition in their respective states, also singled out this defect in the proposed system.[41] It constituted the chief objection of the influential Jefferson, then in France, who let no opportunity fall to make his views known to his numerous correspondents.[42] Accordingly, the lack of a declaration of rights was properly considered by the proponents of the Constitution as the "stronghold" of the Anti-Federalists.[43]

In the Pennsylvania and Virginia Conventions, the arguments on the question were more elaborate and interesting than in any of the others and more attention will conse-

---

[39] The third of those who refused to sign the Constitution was Edmund Randolph, Governor of Virginia, who later became an advocate of ratification. He did not mention the omission of a bill of rights as a defect in his letter to the Virginia House of Delegates in which he explained his action in refusing to sign. Elliot's *Debates*, I, 482.

[40] Letter to the Presiding Officers of the Massachusetts Legislature, in *ibid.*, p. 493. Later, Gerry, writing under the nom de plume "A Columbian Patriot," fittingly epitomized this objection for his state in the following interesting passage: "There is no provision by a bill of rights to guard against the dangerous encroachments of power in too many instances to be named: but I cannot pass over in silence the insecurity in which we are left with regard to warrants unsupported by evidence—the daring experiment of granting *writs of assistance* in a former arbitrary administration is not yet forgotten in the Massachusetts; nor can we be so ungrateful to the memory of the patriots who counteracted their operation, as so soon after their manly exertions to save us from such a detestable instrument of arbitrary power, to subject ourselves to the insolence of any petty revenue officer to enter our houses, search, insult, and seize at pleasure." *Federalist and Other Constitutional Papers*, II, 723. It is interesting to note that the question of search and seizure was the first illustration seized upon by both Lee and Gerry as indicative of the necessity of a bill of rights. Incidentally, this is the only reported instance which has come to the writer's attention where the writ of assistance was used in the discussion rather than general warrants.

[41] *Ibid.*, pp. 651 ff., 688-690. John Lansing, who along with Yates left the Federal Convention long before its adjournment, was the sponsor in the New York Convention of the Bill of Rights recommended to the consideration of a second general convention.

[42] Thorpe, II, 212 ff.; Curtis, *History of the Constitution*, II, 562-563. See also *Writings of Jefferson*, VII, 301, 323.

[43] Ford, *Pamphlets*, p. 241.

quently be given to their proceedings.[44] James Wilson was
the able leader of the Federalist majority in the former. His
principal defense was a classic exposition of the delegated
powers theory, which may be summed up as follows: In set-
ting up the state governments, the people had given up every
power which was not expressly withheld. In the proposed
federal system, however, every power not expressly given was
reserved. It was therefore necessary to prefix bills of rights
to state constitutions,[45] because in order to reserve powers to
the people they had to be specified, whereas the necessity of
this precaution in the Federal Constitution was absent.[46]
Indeed, he continued, a bill of rights was not only unnecessary but dangerous, because a complete list of the rights of
the people was impossible and to stipulate some of them would
be to imply that whatever was not expressed was surren-
dered.[47]

---

[44] The Virginia Convention will be especially considered, since the
question of search and seizure was an important topic of discussion
in that body.

[45] But see his later statement, McMaster and Stone, p. 253.

[46] *Ibid.*, pp. 9-10. Compare his inherent power doctrine, advanced
in 1785, which has become known as the Wilson-Roosevelt doctrine
of construction. See W. W. Willoughby, *Constitutional Law of the
United States* (New York, 1929), I, 80.

[47] *Ibid.*, pp. 254, 261. See further his discussion of the difference
between the situation in England and in this country (p. 249),
which reasoning was also used by Hamilton in the *Federalist*, No. 84,
and Smilie's reply (pp. 249-251); also, in this connection, Bancroft, II, 247.
Of Wilson's argument, which was republished in New York and
Virginia to counteract Lee's insinuations and was widely relied upon
as the best justification for the omission, Bancroft writes: " But
the explanation of the want of a bill of rights satisfied not one state."
Ibid., p. 242. A popular Pennsylvania pamphleteer, " Centinel,"
wrote: " The reason assigned for the omission of a Bill of Rights
. . . is an insult to the understanding of the people." McMaster
and Stone, p. 576. See also Curtis, *History of the Constitution*,
II, 523. Jefferson's views are found quoted in Thorpe, II, 212-213.
The Federalist leaders, who for practical reasons were forced to use
these arguments in defense of the Constitution, seemed to be themselves unconvinced of their validity. Madison, advocating amendments in the First Congress admitted that " some policy has been
made use of, perhaps, by gentlemen on both sides of the question."
He continued: " I am aware that a great number of the most
respectable friends to the Government have thought such a provision
(a bill of rights) not only unnecessary, but even improper; nay,
I believe some have gone, so far as to think it even dangerous."
Annals of Cong., 1st Cong., 1st sess., p. 453. He himself had taken

These arguments were immediately turned against their proponent. It seemed, retorted Mr. Smilie, " that the members of the federal convention were themselves convinced in some degree of the expediency and propriety of a bill of rights, for we find them expressly declaring that the writ of habeas corpus and the trial by jury in criminal cases shall not be suspended or infringed. How does this agree with the maxim that whatever is not given is reserved? " [48] And, said Mr. Whitehill, " I wish it to be seriously considered whether we have a right to leave the liberties of the people to such future constructions and expositions as may possibly be made upon this system; particularly when its advocates, even at this day, confess that it would be dangerous to omit anything in the enumeration of a bill of rights, and according to this principle, the reservation of the habeas corpus, and trial by jury in criminal cases, may hereafter be construed to be the only privileges reserved to the people." [49]

---

this latter position in the Virginia Convention. Elliot's *Debates*, III, 620.

Some of the framers, however, gave full credence to the delegated powers theory. As Washington naïvely wrote to Lafayette, April 28, 1788: " There are many things in the constitution, which only need to be explained, in order to prove equally satisfactory to all parties. For example, there was not a member of the convention, I believe, who had the least objection to what is contended for by the advocates of a Bill of Rights and Trial by Jury. The first, where the people evidently retained everything, which they did not in express terms give up, was considered nugatory. . . ." *Writings of George Washington*, XI, 256. See also, Pierce Butler (member of the Convention) to James Iredell, in Thorpe, II, 224 n.

[48] McMaster and Stone, p. 255.

[49] *Ibid.*, p. 262. The Pennsylvania minority unsuccessfully proposed a Declaration of Rights, article 5 of which prohibited general warrants. *Ibid.*, p. 421. Lee's criticisms, which had circulated in Philadelphia (Bancroft, II, 493; McMaster and Stone, pp. 241, 247), and this Declaration were embodied in an appeal by the minority to their constituents (*ibid.*, pp. 454 ff.) which was widely circulated even as far as down through South Carolina. Pinckney to King, in Warren, p. 766 n.

The few private rights preserved in the Constitution spoiled the whole Federalist case. Grayson and Henry in the Virginia Convention cleverly arrived at a refutation of the entire reserved rights theory, by reasoning that if the privilege of the writ of habeas corpus, for example, had not been stated, then Congress could have suspended it at will, so that the result was that no rights at all were secured unless expressly reserved. Elliot's *Debates*, III, 449, 461. The same could be said of *ex post facto* laws, bills of attainder, and juries in criminal cases.

In Virginia, the vivid and forceful leader of the opposition, Patrick Henry, lost no time in launching an onslaught against this vulnerable point, the subject matter of which was so preeminently fitted for his gift of oratory. Only three days after the opening of the Convention, in the first of his great speeches, he struck the first blow. He dwelt upon the oppressions of state sheriffs and pointed out the greater possibilities in the case of federal sheriffs acting under distant superiors.

When these harpies are aided by excisemen, who may search, at any time, your houses and most secret recesses, will the people bear it? If you think so, you differ from me. Where I thought there was a possibility of such mischiefs, I would grant power with a niggardly hand; and here there is a strong possibility that these oppressions shall actually happen. I may be told that it is safe to err on that side, because such regulations may be made by Congress as shall restrain these officers, and because laws are made by our representatives, and judged by righteous judges: but, sir, as these regulations may be made, so they may not; and many reasons there are to induce a belief that they will not.[50]

Several days later, Mason discussed the potentialities of the "necessary and proper" clause.[51] Thereupon, Henry immediately moved the reading of Articles 8 to 13 of the Virginia Declaration of Rights. Article 10, it will be remembered, prohibited general warrants. Henry's purpose, of course, was to show the connection between the point made by Mason and the consequent insecurity of these liberties under the proposed federal system.[52] A moment later, he entered into a masterfully effective appeal regarding the necessity of a bill of rights. Bills of rights, he argued, were thought necessary in the several state governments and in Virginia.

---

[50] *Ibid.*, p. 58.

[51] *Ibid.*, pp. 441-442. He actually forecast the Alien and Sedition Laws of 1798. See note 23, above.

[52] George Nicholas, the next speaker, retorted: "But why were the articles of the bill of rights read? Let him show us that those rights are given up by the Constitution? Let him prove them to be violated." He then proceeded with the delegated powers argument in all its simplicity: "If I have one thousand acres of land, and I grant five hundred acres of it, must I declare that I retain the other five hundred?" Mason followed with the remark that artful sophistry and evasions could not satisfy him. He could see no clear distinction between rights relinquished by a positive grant, and lost by implication. Unless there were a bill of rights, implication might swallow up all our rights. Elliot's *Debates*, III, 444-445.

Even in the weak Confederation there was an express stipulation that every right was retained by the states which was not delegated to the United States. Why not here when a strong central government was set up? Congress may define crimes and prescribe punishments. The Virginia Bill of Rights provided " that excessive bail ought not to be required nor cruel and unusual punishments inflicted." Under what constitutional restraint would Congress be in this regard? On the question of torture and punishment, why might not Congress introduce the practice of the civil law, where torture to procure a confession is permissible, instead of that of the common law? [53]

They will say that they might as well draw examples from those countries (France, Spain, Germany) as from Great Britain, and they will tell you that there is such a necessity of strengthening the arm of government, that they must have a criminal equity, and extort confession by torture, in order to punish with still more relentless severity. . . . being in a state of uncertainty, they will assume rather than give up power by implication.

. . . In the present Constitution [of Virginia] they [the authorities] are restrained from issuing general warrants to search suspected places, or seize persons not named, without evidence of the commission of a fact, etc. There was certainly some celestial influence governing those who deliberated on that Constitution; for they have, with the most cautious and enlightened circumspection, guarded those indefeasible rights which ought ever to be held sacred! The officers of Congress may come upon you now, fortified with all the terrors of paramount federal authority. Excisemen may come in multitudes; for the limitation of their numbers no man knows. They may, unless the general government be restrained by a bill of rights, or some similar restriction, go into your cellars and rooms, and search, ransack, and measure everything you eat, drink, or wear. They ought to be restrained within proper bounds.[54]

Governor Randolph attempted to meet these arguments by maintaining that they presumed corruption in the government. He said:

That general warrants are grievous and oppressive and ought not to be granted, I fully admit. I heartily concur in expressing my detestation of them. But we have sufficient security here also. We

---

[53] A great deal of the force of Henry's arguments lay in his indulging in particularities, rather than the generalities employed by the defenders of the Constitution.

[54] *Ibid.*, pp. 445-449; Albert J. Beveridge, *Life of John Marshall* (New York, 1916), I, 440. The last mentioned work contains an excellent general description of the proceedings and background of the Virginia Convention.

do not rely on the integrity of any one particular person or body, but on the numbers and different orders of the members of the government—some of them having necessarily the same feelings with ourselves. Can it be believed that the federal judiciary will not be independent enough to prevent such oppressive practices? If they will not do justice to persons injured, may they not go to our own state judiciaries, and obtain it?[55]

When the whole subject had been exhausted, the friends of the Constitution saw that with the parties so nearly equal and with the outcome so doubtful, some concession would have to be made to save the Constitution from defeat either in the form of rejection or of ratification conditional upon previous amendment. The danger and inexpediency of the latter possibility was of course very apparent. Accordingly, George Wythe admitted that the system in certain instances was imperfect and that some amendments were proper. He urged, however, that the critical situation in America and the danger of dissolving the Union rendered it necessary to ratify with recommendations for *subsequent* amendment. He proposed an expression of the principle that every power not granted remained with the people and that among other essential rights, those of liberty of conscience and of the press and trial by jury might not be violated by any authority of the United States.[56]

Henry was immediately upon his feet.

Your subsequent amendments only go to these three amendments. I feel myself distressed, because the necessity of securing our *personal rights* seems not to have pervaded the minds of men; for many other valuable things are omitted:—for instance, general warrants, by which an officer may search suspected places, without evidence of the commission of a fact, or seize any person without evidence of his crime, ought to be prohibited. As these are admitted, any man may be seized, any property may be taken in the most arbitrary manner without any evidence or reason. Everything the most secret may be searched and ransacked by the strong arm of power. We have infinitely more reason to dread general warrants here than they have in England, because there, if a person be confined, liberty may be quickly obtained by the writ of habeas corpus.[57] But here, a man living many hundred miles from the judges may get in prison before he can get that writ.[58]

---

[55] Elliot's *Debates*, III, 468. Aside from the misconceptions of Randolph's argument, it will be noted that its tenor was strictly non-legal and non-constitutional.

[56] *Ibid.*, p. 587.

[57] Henry may here have had the Wilkes case in mind.

[58] *Ibid.*, p. 588. Randolph in reply said: " The honorable gentleman

Henry brought forward a counter-proposal in pursuance of which a declaration of rights and amendments to the most objectionable parts of the Constitution would be referred to the other states for consideration prior to ratification. This was defeated by a narrow margin and instead a committee was appointed to prepare *recommendatory* amendments.[59] These were nearly the same as those previously advocated by Henry and were adopted later by the Convention.[60] The fourteenth section of a lengthy bill of rights treated the subject of search and seizure, a subject which had occupied a very prominent place in the debates in the Convention.[61] The provision was

---

says there is no restraint on the power of issuing general warrants. If I be tedious in asking where is that power, you will ascribe it to him who has put me in the necessity of asking. They have no such power given them: if they have, where is it? " *Ibid.*, p. 600.

[59] This committee of 20 included Wythe, Henry, Randolph, Mason, Madison, and Marshall.

[60] *Ibid.*, pp. 593, 657-661. As to the amendments proposed, the representatives of Virginia in Congress were enjoined " to exert all their influence, and use all reasonable and legal methods to obtain ratification." (p. 661.)

[61] " 14th. That every freeman has a right to be secure from all unreasonable searches and seizures of his person, his papers, and property; all warrants, therefore, to search suspected places, or seize any freeman, his papers, or property, without information on oath (or affirmation of a person religiously scrupulous of taking an oath) of legal and sufficient cause, are grievous and oppressive; and all general warrants to search suspected places, or to apprehend any suspected person, without specially naming or describing the place or person, are dangerous, and ought not to be granted." *Ibid.*, p. 658. Note the limitation of the first two clauses to freemen, while the prohibition as to general warrants is made universal. Whether any distinction was actually intended is uncertain. However, in the Declaration of Rights recommended by the New York Convention a month later, which showed a marked similarity on the whole to that of Virginia, the search and seizure provision was modelled closely after the Virginia phraseology and retained the word " freemen "; but peculiarly, whereas the Virginia document had used the term in connection with a number of rights, this was the only provision of the New York bill which restricted the right to that class. The " people " and " all persons " were declared entitled to the other rights enumerated. This phraseology was probably the inadvertent result of modelling after the Virginia wording without noticing the inconsistency. On the other hand, in the rights declared by Rhode Island upon its ratification of the Constitution in 1790, almost every one of the Virginia recommendations were copied verbatim, and yet in the search and seizure provisions, which was otherwise taken word for word from the New York provision, pains were deliberately taken to substitute " person " for " freeman."

broader than the analogous clause in the Virginia Bill of
Rights which had only concerned itself with general warrants.
The proposed section added the principle of security from
unreasonable search and seizure and also the necessity of oath
or affirmation.[62]

---

[62] Delaware, Pennsylvania, New Jersey, Connecticut, Georgia,
Massachusetts, Maryland, South Carolina, and New Hampshire,
which comprised the necessary nine states to put the Constitution
into effect, had, in the order named, already ratified before Virginia.
Of all the thirteen original ·states, the first five listed above and
Maryland completed the list of those ratifying without asking for
amendments.   In some of these, for example Pennsylvania and
Maryland, dissatisfied minorities were persistent in demanding
amendments to the Constitution.
    In Maryland, a committee appointed to prepare amendments
adhered closely to the provision in the Maryland Declaration of
Rights as regards search and seizure. See note 12, above. A report
of the committee's deliberations states the following: " This amendment was considered indispensable by many of the Committee; for
Congress having the power of laying excises (the horror of a free
people), by which our dwelling houses, those castles considered so
sacred by the English law, will be laid open to the insolence and
oppression of office, there could be no constitutional check provided
that would prove so effectual a safeguard to our citizens.   General
warrants, too, the great engine by which power may destroy those
individuals who resist usurpation, are also hereby forbidden to those
magistrates who are to administer the general government." Subsequently, however, the controlling Federalist majority decided as a
matter of policy not to advocate any amendments at all so as to give
the approbation of the state the most favorable aspect possible in
view of the approaching struggles in the pivotal states.   Elliot's
Debates, II, 547-556.
    As regards a bill of rights, Massachusetts and South Carolina
in their recommendations were content with a mere formal statement
that powers not expressly delegated were retained by the states.
Samuel Adams acknowledged himself satisfied with this stipulation
as a summary of a bill of rights. Ibid., I, 322, 325; II, 131, see
also, letters from Lee to Adams in Ballagh,.II, 445, 457; also E. P.
Smith, " Second Constitutional Convention," in J. F. Jameson's
Essays on Constitutional History (Boston, 1889), p. 69; Curtis, Constitutional History, II, 530-540.   New Hampshire, although a few
of its recommendations were properly referable to a bill of rights,
was also satisfied with a like general stipulation as security for other
rights. Elliot's Debates, I, 325-327. In New York, the Constitution
was ratified with what almost amounted to a qualified ratification,
and a lengthy Declaration of Rights and numerous amendments were
referred to the consideration of a proposed second general convention,
the assembling of which was superseded by the passage by Congress
of the first amendments. Curtis, Constitutional History, II, 585-591;
Elliot's Debates, I, 327-331. See note 61, above.
    North Carolina and Rhode Island had not yet ratified when the
new government began functioning in 1789.   The North Carolina
Convention neither ratified nor rejected.   A Bill of Rights and
amendments were recommended to the consideration of Congress or of

It was principally the realization of the benefits of union and the inexpediency of disunion and not a mutual regard for the merits of the new scheme of government that ultimately led to the adoption of the Constitution. The general view, however, is that the Constitution would never have been ratified *even then* but for the tacit understanding that it would be amended so as to embody the customary guaranties of personal liberty.[63]

The Federal Government began functioning in an atmosphere of doubt and apprehension. Two states were still out of the Union. Five of the more important had ratified asking for amendment in some respects. Several advocated a second general convention. And popular unrest and dissatisfaction were prevalent everywhere. Thus, Washington adverted to the necessity of amendments no later than in his inaugural address to both houses of Congress. He indicated, however, that he favored no radical alteration of the Constitution and recommended simply the safeguarding of "the characteristic rights of freemen" in order advantageously to promote public harmony.[64]

Madison was the sponsor of the first amendments through Congress. The impression had been spread in his district by his opponents that he was opposed to amendments [65] and he thus had had to pledge himself openly to their support

a second convention to be called. This Bill of Rights was a verbatim reproduction of the Virginia recommendations, with the *single* exception, strangely, of the search and seizure provision, which was passed deleted of the " oath or affirmation " clause. The only apparent reason for this was that the kindred provision in the state constitution was also silent on that score. Elliot's *Debates*, IV, 243 ff. The legislature of Rhode Island, in which state there was a high spirit of individual and public independence, submitted the Constitution to the freemen in their town meetings, where it was rejected. No convention was called until March, 1790. Curtis, *Constitutional History*, II, 598-603.

[63] Davis, J., in *Ex parte Milligan*, 4 Wall. 2, 120 (1866) ; John A. Jameson, *Constitutional Convention*, p. 91; Warren, p. 510.

[64] James D. Richardson (ed.), *Messages and Papers of the Presidents* (Washington, 1896), I, 45; *Writings of George Washington*, XI, 385-386. For the replies of the Senate and the House, see Richardson, I, 47, 48.

[65] Madison to Washington, January 14, 1789, in *Writings of Madison*, V, 319 ff.

in order to secure his election.[66] He had, of course, opposed ratification conditional upon amendments. Now that the Constitution was ratified, however, he felt that amending it would serve the double purpose of satisfying the minds of well-meaning opponents and of providing additional guards in favor of liberty, although he freely acknowledged that he did not see the dangers of infringement of these rights by the government that others did.[67] Yet it was indeed fortunate that a man of Madison's influence and ability was behind the movement for amendments, for the Federalist majority in Congress gave the whole program a cold reception. It was only by persistent effort that even Madison finally accomplished what he did.[68]

On May 4, 1789, four days after Washington's inauguration, Madison had already given notice of his intention to bring up the subject of amendments.[69] This was the day before the introduction of the petition of the General Assembly of Virginia requesting Congress to call a second general convention.[70] The question came up for discussion on June 8. After pointing out the prevailing dissatisfaction and the desirability of appeasing it if that could be done by amendments of such a nature as would not injure the Constitution, Madison went on to say:

But perhaps there is a stronger motive than this for our going into a consideration of the subject. It is to provide those securities for liberty which are required by a part of the community; I allude in a particular manner to those two States that have not thought fit to throw themselves into the bosom of the Confederacy. . . . I have no doubt, if we proceed to take those steps which would be prudent, and requisite at this juncture, that in a short time we should see that disposition prevailing in those States which have embraced the constitution.[71]

---

[66] W. W. Henry, *Patrick Henry* (New York, 1891), II, 441.

[67] Madison to Eve, January 2, 1789, in *Writings of Madison*, V, 320. For a very interesting comparison of the views of Madison and Jefferson, see their correspondence in *ibid.*, pp. 271 ff.; *Writings of Jefferson*, VII, 309 ff.

[68] William C. Rives, *History of the Life and Times of James Madison* (Boston, 1873), III, 40-44. See the attempts to delay and postpone in *Annals of Cong.*, 1st Cong., 1st sess., pp. 441, 685-690, 732-734.

[69] *Ibid.*, p. 257.   [70] *Ibid.*, pp. 258 ff.

[71] *Ibid.*, p. 449. See also the speech by Gerry, pp. 463 ff.

He admitted that many of the rights respecting which the American people were most alarmed were not contained in any of the great documents in English constitutional history.[72] But the people of this country were agreed that barriers against legislative power and, for that matter, against all governmental power were necessary.[73]

So much for the practical side of his argument. It was still essential to refute the idea that a bill of rights was unnecessary because of the theory of delegated and reserved powers, of which theory he himself had previously been an advocate. Here he showed the influence of the debate in the Virginia Convention the year before.

It is true, the powers of the General Government are circumscribed, they are directed to particular objects; but even if [the] Government keeps within those limits, it has certain discretionary powers with respect to the means, which may admit of abuse to a certain extent, in the same manner as the powers of the State Governments under their constitutions may to an indefinite extent; because in the constitution of the United States, there is a clause granting to Congress the power to make all laws which shall be necessary and proper for carrying into execution all the powers vested in the Government of the United States, or in any department or officer thereof; this enables them to fulfill every purpose for which the Government was established. Now, may not laws be considered necessary and proper by Congress, for it is for them to judge of the necessity and propriety to accomplish those special purposes which they may have in contemplation, which laws in themselves are neither necessary nor proper; as well as improper laws could be enacted by the State Legislatures, for fulfilling the more extended objects of those Governments. I will state an instance, which I think in point, and proves that this might be the case. The General Government has a right to pass all laws which shall be necessary to collect its revenue; the means for enforcing the collection are within the discretion of the Legislature; may not general warrants be considered necessary for this purpose, as well as for some purposes which it was supposed at the framing of their constitutions the State Governments had in view? If there was reason for restraining the State Governments from exercising this power, there is like reason for restraining the Federal Government.[74]

---

[72] Madison must have mentioned general warrants somewhere in this connection, for we find a reference to them at this point in the notes that he used in delivering his address. *Writings of Madison,* V, 389.

[73] *Annals of Cong.,* 1st Cong., 1st sess., pp. 453-454.

[74] *Ibid.,* pp. 455-456. It is interesting to note that general warrants were to him the most prominent illustration (as it was to others, e. g., Gerry, note 40, above) of the need of a bill of rights. Note also the similarity of the reasoning used by Warren (note 23, above). Madison had shown the importance with which he regarded the ques-

Madison made nine proposals.[75] The essence of the short bill
of rights finally adopted was contained in his fourth proposition,[76] of which the eighth clause was the search and seizure
provision. The wording of this clause was such that it
seemed to be directed against improper warrants only.[77]
Madison's propositions were referred on July 21 to a Committee of Eleven made up of one member from each state.[78]
On August 13, the House resolved itself into a Committee of
the Whole to consider the report and the debate upon the
proposed amendments, each being considered separately, lasted
ten days.[79]

tion of search and seizure in a letter to George Eve, January 2, 1789,
in which he stated: " It is my sincere opinion that the Constitution
ought to be revised, and that the first Congress meeting under it
ought to prepare and recommend to the states for ratification the
most satisfactory provisions for all essential rights, particularly the
rights of conscience in the fullest latitude, the freedom of the press,
trials by jury, security against general warrants, etc." *Writings of
Madison*, V, 320. These provisions seemed to be uppermost in his
mind.

[75] *Annals of Cong.*, 1st Cong., 1st sess., pp. 451-453. Madison did
not advocate all the recommendations of Virginia. As a matter of
policy he hazarded nothing which would cause too much controversy.
" Two or three contentious additions would, even now, prostrate the
whole project." Madison to Randolph, *Documentary History of the
Constitution*, V, 191. As it was, a good portion of what he supported
was not successful, especially in the Senate.

[76] Madison intended to insert all the amendments into the Constitution itself and the opinion of the House was agreeable to this
for some time. If this plan had been carried out, most of the ten
amendments ultimately adopted, including the fourth, would have
been in Article I, Section 9, between clauses 3 and 4. See Thorpe,
II, 228-232, 250.

[77] " The rights of the people to be secured in their persons, their
houses, their papers, and their other property, from all unreasonable
searches and seizures, shall not be violated by warrants issued
without probable cause, supported by oath or affirmation, or not
particularly describing the places to be searched, or the persons or
things to be seized." *Annals of Cong.*, 1st Cong., 1st sess., p. 452.
It became the seventh clause of the fourth proposition in the report
of the Committee of Eleven.

The observation may be made that the language of the proposal
did not purport to *create* the right to be secure from unreasonable
searches and seizures but merely stated it as a right which already
existed.

[78] *Ibid.*, p. 690.

[79] For a review of the passage of the amendments from the standpoint of the Judiciary Act of 1789, see Charles Warren, " The
Judiciary Act of 1789," *Harvard Law Review*, 1923, XXXVII, 111 ff.

The most interesting thing about the passage of the Fourth Amendment to the Constitution, if we are to rely upon available records, is that the House seems never to have consciously agreed to the Amendment in its present form. As a matter of fact, and this is the important thing, the House actually voted down a motion to make it read as it does now. The Committee of Eleven had reported the provision as follows:

> The right of the people to be secured in their persons, houses, papers, and effects, shall not be violated by warrants issuing without probable cause, supported by oath or affirmation, and not particularly describing the place to be searched, and the persons or things to be seized.

After Gerry had noted the mistake in phraseology and had had it corrected to read " the right of the people to be *secure* in their persons, houses, papers, and effects, against unreasonable searches and seizures," the following took place:

> Mr. Benson objected to the words " by warrants issuing." This declaratory provision was good as far as it went, but he thought it was not sufficient; he therefore proposed to alter it so as to read " and no warrant shall issue."
> The question was put on this motion, and lost by a considerable majority.[80]

However, on August 24, when Benson as chairman of a Committee of Three, which had been appointed to arrange the amendments,[81] reported an arrangement of the amendments as they were supposed to have been agreed upon by the House, the *clause appeared as he had proposed it and as the House had rejected it.*[82]

And so it stands today.[83] The records do not show that the

---

[80] *Annals of Cong.*, 1st Cong., 1st sess., p. 783. The only other point raised was this: " Mr. Livermore objected to the words ' and not ' between ' affirmation ' and ' particularly.' He moved to strike them out, in order to make it an affirmative proposition. But the motion passed in the negative." See also *ibid.*, p. 796.

[81] The committee was composed of Benson (N. Y.), Sherman (Conn.), and Sedgwick (Mass.). For other activities of Sherman, see pages 73, 84 ff., above.

[82] *House Journal*, August 24, 1789.

[83] That this radical change took place in the Committee of Three has also been noted, but without further remark, by Osmand K. Fraenkel in his article " Concerning Searches and Seizures," *Harvard Law Review*, 1921, XXXIV, 366, n. 30.

alteration was ever noticed or assented to as such by the House.[84] In this form it was received and agreed to by the Senate.[85] And the only remaining discussion by the House and Senate concerned those amendments upon which the two houses were not in accord.[86]

It cannot be maintained, however, that the Fourth Amendment as it is now worded is not properly a part of the Constitution. It was accepted by the Senate, later formally

---

[84] The writer has attempted to verify the vote on Benson's motion as reported in the *Annals of Congress* (Gales and Seaton). The only other record of the debates of this session seems to be Thomas Lloyd's *The Congressional Register* (New York, 1790), where the same result is found (II, 266). Closer investigation shows, however, that the Gales and Seaton edition, which was published in 1834 and " compiled from authentic materials," was a reprint of Lloyd, so that the latter does not serve as an independent source, except to show that no typographical error was made in the *Annals*. There is, however, no reason to believe that Lloyd, who was present during the session and took shorthand notes, erred in reporting the proceedings, especially since his attentiveness is indicated by his remarking that the motion was not merely lost, but that it was *lost by a considerable majority*. It should also be observed that Benson had been a member of the Committee of Eleven to which the proposals had been referred for consideration, and that he had presumably advocated and discussed his reasons for the same change in committee, but without avail. He may here, in the House, again have been trying to have the alteration made, this time against the report of the committee.

[85] *Senate Journal*, August 25, 1789.

[86] Little information concerning the deliberations of the Senate is available, due to the fact that until 1794 the Senate sat behind closed doors and that there are consequently no reports of its debates. The *Journal of William MacClay* (New York, 1927), the most useful of the secondary sources to the proceedings, contains only passing mention of the arrival of the amendments in the Senate on August 25. MacClay was ill and unable to attend during the discussion of the amendments (pp. 131, 141-148). The Senate debated them from September 2 to September 9, during which time the Virginia senators attempted unsuccessfully to introduce the other Virginia recommendations. See their letters to Patrick Henry, in Henry, III, 391-392, 399, 402-403, 406. The seventeen articles which the House had agreed upon (of which the search and seizure provision was Article VII) were, in a number of instances, objected to by the Senate, modified, and returned to the House, which held its ground. A conference committee was then appointed to reach some form of agreement. Each house receded partly from its previous position and on September 25 twelve articles (Article VII had become Article VI) were adopted and submitted to the states, including North Carolina and Rhode Island.

enacted by both houses of Congress,[87] and so ratified by the states. But the reason behind the present phraseology is still important. As reported by the Committee of Eleven and corrected by Gerry, the Amendment was a one-barrelled affair, directed apparently only to the essentials of a valid warrant. The general principle of freedom from unreasonable search and seizure seems to have been stated only by way of premise, and the positive inhibition upon action by the Federal Government limited consequently to the issuance of warrants without probable cause, etc. That Benson interpreted it in this light is shown by his argument that although the clause was good as far as it went, *it was not sufficient,* and by the change which he advocated to obviate this objection.[88] The provision as he proposed it contained *two* clauses. The general right of security from unreasonable search and seizure was given a sanction of its own and the amendment thus intentionally given a broader scope. That the prohibition against " unreasonable searches " was intended, accordingly, to cover something other than the form of the warrant is a question no longer left to implication to be derived from the phraseology of the Amendment.[89]

The passage of the first ten amendments had the desired and anticipated effect. In the first place, the strength and unity of the parties which were adverse to the Constitution were greatly disrupted. In the second place, the dangerous possibilities attending a second constitutional convention were avoided. And, in the third place, the amendments were a factor in bringing into the Union soon afterwards the two

---

[87] *Documentary History of the Constitution*, II, 321.

[88] In his review of the passage of the amendments, Thorpe totally overlooks the point and substance of Benson's proposal, together with the inconsistency of the defeat of his motion and the present wording of the Fourth Amendment. He writes: " Benson objected to the words ' by warrants issuing ' and wished them changed to the simpler form, ' no warrant shall issue,' but was not successful; the committee of the whole finally adopting the clause with Gerry's amendment of its language."　Thorpe, II, 245.

[89] Cf. Fraenkel, *Harvard Law Review*, XXXIV, 366. Cf. also such cases as *Boyd* v. *United States*, 116 U. S. 616, 29 L. ed. 746, 6 Sup. Ct. 524 (1886) ; *Hale* v. *Henkel*, 201 U. S. 43, 50 L. ed. 652, 26 Sup. Ct. 370 (1906).

recalcitrant states. The mere knowledge that Congress intended to submit a number of amendments which would remove many objections had already served to change public sentiment in North Carolina,[90] so that less than two months after the submission of the amendments to the states a second convention was called and the Constitution adopted. North Carolina thus was the twelfth state to enter the Union and the third to ratify the amendments. Rhode Island, where the opposition was still great, was not far behind. The legislature had seven times refused to call a convention to consider the Constitution. Satisfaction was indicated, however, upon the passage of the amendments [91] and finally, after considerable pressure had been brought to bear by Congress and the press, a convention was called which adopted the Constitution by a vote of 34 to 32, in May, 1790.[92] The legislature later ratified the proposed amendments. Rhode Island being the ninth state to ratify, the amendments thereupon became part of the Constitution.[93]

The reaction to the adoption of the amendments was immediate. The popularity of the Constitution increased tremendously. As history has shown, it was indeed fortunate for

[90] Thorpe, II, 181, 185.

[91] See the memorial which Rhode Island sent to the President and Congress, September, 1789, in Herman V. Ames, *State Documents on Federal Relations* (Philadelphia, 1906), p. 3.

[92] The Convention recommended a Bill of Rights, a good number of the provisions of which were already in the proposals submitted by Congress. Elliot's *Debates*, I, 334 ff. The reason for this repetition is not clear. See also note 61, above.

[93] The formal ratifications of the states may be found in *Documentary History of the Constitution*, II, 325 ff. The first two articles proposed by Congress, relating to representation and increases in salaries of senators and representatives, were never ratified by a sufficient number of states. Article VI thereupon became Amendment IV.

Every state which ratified any of the amendments, ratified the search and seizure provision. Thorpe is again in error when he states (II, 263) that it was rejected along with other articles by Maryland. That state ratified all the propositions submitted. This oversight is probably due to the peculiar arrangement of the amendments as returned by Maryland. See *Documentary History of the Constitution*, II, 330 ff.

The records of the Department of State do not show that Massachusetts, Connecticut, or Georgia ever made any returns.

the new Union, which was soon again torn with so much dissension, that this should be so. The leaders who had opposed the Constitution were still dissatisfied, for they had insisted upon changes in its framework as well. But their strongest bid for popular support was gone. They could no longer appeal to that defect in the new régime which the public in general could most appreciate and understand. Without this popular support, the backbone of the forces arrayed against the Constitution was broken.

"The amendments once ratified," states one writer, "all notes of opposition were lost in the chorus of admiration that resounded from every quarter. In the worship of the Constitution that instantly succeeded, men forgot that it had been 'extorted from the grinding necessity of a reluctant people.' . . . It was almost impossible to believe that an instrument, accepted by all parties as the last word of political wisdom, had been produced in a conflict of opinion, adopted with doubt, ratified with hesitation, and amended with difficulty."[94]

---

[94] Smith, in Jameson's *Essays in Constitutional History*, pp. 114-115.

CHAPTER IV

DEVELOPMENT OF THE PRINCIPLE BY THE SUPREME COURT

It is not surprising to find that during the century following the adoption of the Federal Constitution and its first ten amendments only a few cases involving interpretation of the Fourth Amendment reached the Supreme Court.[1] During this period, the limited criminal jurisdiction of the Federal Government was not exercised by Congress except in minor instances. Later on, after the passage of the Interstate Commerce Act in 1887 and the Sherman Anti-Trust Law in 1890, a series of cases arose involving the question whether the compulsory production of papers by legal process violated the Amendment. But finally, with the extension of the criminal jurisdiction of the United States over such matters as the sale of narcotics and intoxicating liquors, the Fourth Amendment became one of the most prominent and litigated provisions of the Bill of Rights. All in all, more than seventy cases that have had to do with the interpretation of the Amendment have reached the Supreme Court.

Several of the earlier cases may be quickly reviewed.[2]

---

[1] It is interesting to note that in early cases the Fourth Amendment was cited as Amendment 6, because it stood sixth in the list of amendments as they were submitted to the states for ratification. The first two never were ratified. See *Ex parte Burford*, 3 Cr. 448, 2 L. ed. 495 (1860); *United States* v. *Bollman*, Fed. Cas. 14,622 (1807).

[2] Cf. the cases cited in the note above and also *Ex parte Bollman and Swartwout*, 4 Cr. 75, 2 L. ed. 554 (1807).

In *Luther* v. *Borden*, 7 How. 1, 12 L. ed. 581 (1849), Chief Justice Taney held that when martial law was declared, military officers might lawfully arrest anyone who from information before them they have reasonable grounds to believe is engaged in insurrection, and may order a house to be forcibly entered and searched when there are reasonable grounds to suppose that he is there concealed. Cf. the dissenting opinion of Mr. Justice Woodbury.

Where martial law does not exist or cannot be legally declared, the Fourth Amendment and other provisions of the Bill of Rights cannot in any way be infringed on the ground of some emergency, according to *Ex parte Milligan*, 4 Wall. 2, 18 L. ed. 281 (1866). On this point see the language of Cranch, C. J., in *United States* v. *Bollman*, cit. above, with which compare that of Mr. Justice Holmes in *Schenck* v. *United States*, 249 U. S. 47, 63 L. ed. 470, 39 Sup. Ct. 247 (1919).

In *Smith* v. *Maryland*, 18 How. 71, 15 L. ed. 269 (1855), the

The Court held in 1855, in the case of *Murray* v. *Hoboken Land Company,*[3] that the Fourth Amendment applied to criminal proceedings only and had no relation to civil proceedings for the recovery of debts.[4] Consequently, a distress warrant issued by a solicitor of the Treasury against a delinquent tax collector was not invalid because it was not under oath. In the case of *In re Jackson,*[5] decided in 1877, it was held that letters and packages in the mail that were closed to inspection could not be opened without a search warrant.[6]

The first case of real importance was decided in 1886. This was *Boyd* v. *United States,*[7] one of the leading cases on the subject of search and seizure, a case which did much to chart the subsequent course of the federal law. By an act of Congress, it had been provided that in forfeiture proceedings under the revenue laws, the district attorney might move the court to issue a notice to the defendants requiring the production of any records desirable for the prosecution of the case. The penalty for not producing such records was that any allegations the district attorney might make as to what these records contained would be taken as confessed.

Court held, under the well-settled rule that the first eight amendments of the Constitution apply to the Federal Government only, that the Fourth Amendment had no application to state process.' The applicability in this regard of the Fourteenth Amendment will be mentioned later.

[3] 18 How. 272, 15 L. ed. 372 (1855).

[4] See also *Boyd* v. *United States,* 116 U. S. 616, 29 L. ed. 746, 6 Sup. Ct. 524 (1886); *Fong Yue Ting* v. *United States,* 149 U. S. 698, 37 L. ed. 905, 13 Sup. Ct. 1016 (1892); *American Tobacco Co.* v. *Werckmeister,* 207 U. S. 284, 52 L. ed. 208, 28 Sup. Ct. 72 (1907); *Blackmer* v. *United States,* 284 U. S. 421, 76 L. ed. 375, 52 Sup. Ct. 252 (1932).

[5] 96 U. S. 727, 24 L. ed. 877 (1877).

[6] This holding in the case was really *obiter dictum.*

Where letters were written by a person in prison, however, and came into the hands of the prison officials under the established practice of examining such letters, which practice was reasonably warranted in order to promote discipline, the Supreme Court has held that the opening of the letters did not require a warrant and that the use of the letters as evidence against the prisoner did not constitute a violation of the Fifth Amendment as regards self-incrimination. *Stroud* v. *United States,* 251 U. S. 15, 64 L. ed. 103, 40 Sup. Ct. 50 (1919).

[7] Cit. above.

The defendants in the *Boyd* case brought into court the invoice required by the notice that was issued but objected to the validity of the notice and the law which sanctioned it. The Court upheld their contention that the statute and notice were unconstitutional as violations of both the Fourth Amendment and that part of the Fifth Amendment which provides that no person " shall be compelled in any criminal case to be a witness against himself."

With regard to the Fourth Amendment, wrote Mr. Justice Bradley in this much-quoted opinion, it is true that the statute did not authorize the search and seizure of books and papers but only required the defendant to produce them. But the stipulation that the non-production of the documents required would result in a confession of the allegations that the prosecutor affirmed they would prove was tantamount to compelling their production, for the district attorney would always be sure to state the evidence expected to be derived from them as strongly as the case would permit. It was the opinion of the Court, therefore, " that a compulsory production of a man's private papers to establish a criminal charge against him or to forfeit his property is within the scope of the Fourth Amendment to the Constitution in all cases in which a search and seizure would be; because it is a material ingredient and effects the whole object and purpose of search and seizure."

This being a search and seizure then, was it an unreasonable search and seizure within the prohibition of the Constitution? In the first place, said the Court, the property which may be searched for and seized must be such that the government or other claimant is entitled to its possession, or to which the defendant is not entitled, such as stolen goods, gambling implements, counterfeit coin, etc. Search warrants may be used for these things but this is entirely different from a search for and seizure of a man's private books and papers in order to get information therein contained or to use them in evidence against him. In the famous case of

Entick v. *Carrington*,[8] indeed, Lord Camden in denouncing the general warrant to search for papers had tied up search for such evidence with the privilege against self-incrimination, holding that the latter was another reason why such search was illegal. The principles laid down in this case, said Mr. Justice Bradley, apply broadly " to all invasions, on the part of the Government and its employees, of the sanctity of a man's home and the privacies of life. It is not the breaking of his doors and the rummaging of his drawers that constitute the essence of the offense; but it is the invasion of his indefeasible right of personal security, personal liberty, and private property, where that right has never been forfeited by his conviction of some public offense."

Thus, the Fourth and Fifth Amendments are intimately connected, the Court continued, and throw great light upon each other.

> For the 'unreasonable searches and seizures' condemned in the Fourth Amendment are almost always made for the purpose of compelling a man to give evidence against himself, which in criminal cases is condemned in the Fifth Amendment; and compelling a man 'in a criminal case to be a witness against himself' which is condemned in the Fifth Amendment, throws light on the question as to what is an 'unreasonable search and seizure' within the meaning of the Fourth Amendment. And we have been unable to perceive that the seizure of a man's private books and papers to be used in evidence against him is substantially different from compelling him to be a witness against himself. We think it is the clear intent and meaning of those terms.[9]

The Court closed with an eloquent appeal for a liberal, and not merely a literal, construction of the amendments. This is a rule of interpretation to which the Supreme Court has

---

[8] *State Trials*, XIX, 1029 (1765). See pages 47-48, above, for a discussion of this case.

[9] Mr. Justice Miller wrote a concurring opinion, in which he was supported by Chief Justice Waite, wherein he maintained that since there was no actual search and seizure, the Fourth Amendment was inapplicable, and that therefore the case should have been governed by the Fifth Amendment alone. There is much force to this argument. For other criticisms, see John H. Wigmore, " Using Evidence Obtained by Illegal Search and Seizure," *American Bar Association Journal*, 1922, VIII, 479; Senator Knute Nelson, " Search and Seizure: *Boyd* vs. *United States*," *ibid.*, 1923, IX, 773. See also Edward S. Corwin, " The Supreme Court's Construction of the Self-Incrimination Clause," *Michigan Law Review*, 1930, XXIX, 1, 191.

always adhered, at least in terms, in construing the guaranties of personal liberty contained in the Constitution.[10]

Seventeen years later, however, in *Adams* v. *New York*,[11] the Supreme Court handed down an opinion which seemed effectively to overrule the doctrine of the *Boyd* case. In this case several policemen acting under a warrant to search for policy gambling slips in the office of the defendant, entered the office, arrested the defendant upon his arrival a little later on, and seized not only the gambling slips but also other papers which were not mentioned in the warrant. The defendant objected to the admissibility of these papers as evidence against him when they were offered during his trial. The Supreme Court held upon appeal from the state court that the search for and seizure of the papers had not been unreasonable,[12] but held also that the evidence was admissible *even if there had been an unreasonable search and seizure,* basing its decision on the common law rule that courts will not stop during the trial of a case and create a collateral issue by instituting an inquiry into the means by

---

[10] The following language of this opinion has been often referred to in other cases: "Though the proceeding in question is divested of many of the aggravating incidents of actual search and seizure, yet, as before said, it contains their substance and essence, and effects their substantial purpose. It may be that it is the obnoxious thing in its mildest and least repulsive form; but illegal practices get their first footing in that way; namely, by silent approaches and slight deviations from legal modes of procedure. This can only be obviated by adhering to the rule that constitutional provisions for the security of person and property should be liberally construed. A close and literal construction deprives them of half their efficacy and leads to gradual depreciation of the right, as if it consisted more in sound than in substance. It is the duty of courts to be watchful for the constitutional rights of the citizen, and against any stealthy encroachments thereon. Their motto should be *obsta principiis.*" See also *Gouled* v. *United States*, 255 U. S. 298, 65 L. ed. 647, 41 Sup. Ct. 261 (1921); *Federal Trade Commission* v. *American Tobacco Co.*, 264 U. S. 298, 68 L. ed. 696, 44 Sup. Ct. 336, 32 A. L. R. 786 (1924); *Go-Bart Importing Co.* v. *United States*, 282 U. S. 344, 75 L. ed. 374, 51 Sup. Ct. 153 (1932); *United States* v. *Lefkowitz*, 285 U. S. 452, 76 L. ed. 877, 52 Sup. Ct. 420 (1932); *Grau* v. *United States*, 287 U. S. 124, 77 L. ed. 212, 53 Sup. Ct. 38 (1932).

[11] 192 U. S. 585, 48 L. ed. 575, 24 Sup. Ct. 372 (1903).

[12] Cf. *Go-Bart Importing Co.* v. *United States*, cit. above; *United States* v. *Lefkowitz*, cit. above.

which evidence which is otherwise admissible has been acquired. According to this holding, then, it seemed that evidence procured by a violation of the Fourth Amendment, although this Amendment was not involved in the case, could still be introduced against the person whose rights had been infringed.[13]

But in 1914, in the case of *Weeks* v. *United States*,[14] the Court limited the decision in the *Adams* case without overruling it, so as to give the defendant against whom evidence had been seized in violation of his constitutional rights the opportunity of asserting them. In this case the defendant was charged with having used the mails to transmit lottery tickets in violation of federal law. He was arrested at his place of employment, the officers went to his room, searched it without a search warrant of any kind, and carried away everything from money to clothing, including certain letters and other incriminating evidence. But prior to the time for trial, the defendant came into court and *petitioned for the return of his property* on the ground that it had been illegally seized. The trial court returned only those articles which were not necessary for the prosecution and at the trial, over defendant's objection, admitted the incriminating evidence.

Upon these facts, the Supreme Court held, in an opinion by Mr. Justice Day—who incidentally had also rendered the opinion in the *Adams* case—that the search was clearly illegal and that permitting the evidence thus obtained to come in, after the defendant had petitioned for its return before trial, was a violation of the self-incrimination clause of the Fifth Amendment. The Court reiterated the position taken in the *Adams* case but held that the defendant had avoided creating a collateral issue during the progress of the trial by

[13] Since the Court held that there had been no unreasonable search and seizure and consequently no self-incrimination in the case, it found it unnecessary to decide whether the Fourth and Fifth Amendments were privileges and immunities of citizens of the United States as to bind the state of New York under the Fourteenth Amendment.

[14] 232 U. S. 383, 58 L. ed. 652, 34 Sup. Ct. 341, L. R. A. 1915 B 834, Ann. Cas. 1915 C 117 (1914).

requesting the return of the property *before* the trial, when
the question could have been settled without interrupting the
course of the proceedings.[15]

⟨In subsequent cases the Court has gone even farther in
limiting the collateral issue doctrine, although it still up-
holds it, and has reasonably extended the theory of the *Weeks*
case to meet other circumstances. So in *Gouled* v. *United
States*,[16] where the defendant had no knowledge of an illegal
seizure of certain papers by a government investigator who
had taken them by stealth from his home, first becoming
aware of the fact of the seizure when the evidence was introduced against him at the trial, it was held that an objection
made at the time the evidence was offered could not in fair-
ness be said to have come too late since the defendant had no
prior opportunity to move for its suppression and return.[16a]
While the collateral issue rule, said Mr. Justice Clarke, " is

---

[15] Cf. Albert J. Harno, " Evidence Obtained by Illegal Search and
Seizure," *Illinois Law Review*, 1925, XIX, 303, 312.

This method of circumventing the decision in the *Adams* case had
already been successfully practiced in the lower federal courts. In
the first case in which this procedure was approved and a motion
granted for a return of the evidence, *United States* v. *Mills*, 185
Fed. 318 (1911), it is interesting to note that the district attorney,
apparently confident of his ground because of the decision in the
Adams case, refused to obey the order of the court and was held in
contempt. He appealed to the Supreme Court, which ruled against
him, denying jurisdiction on a procedural ground. *Wise* v. *Mills*,
220 U. S. 556, 55 L. ed. 581, 31 Sup. Ct. 599 (1911).

[16] 255 U. S. 298, 65 L. ed. 647, 41 Sup. Ct. 261 (1921).

[16a] See also *Agnello* v. *United States*, 269 U. S. 20, 70 L. ed. 145,
46 Sup. Ct. 4, 51 A. L. R. 409 (1925). The Court also held in the
Gouled case that where a motion is made before trial for the return
of the evidence on the ground of an unconstitutional seizure, and
the motion is denied, but in the progress of the trial it becomes
probable that the seizure has been unconstitutional, the trial court
must entertain an objection to its admission as then presented. This
ruling is an obviously proper one, since the defendant has done all
he can to prevent a collateral issue by bringing up the question
before trial and the court should not be allowed to make its own
error the pretext for refusing to reconsider the point.

Where the court has gone so far as to err in admitting the evidence, then it can still cure this error by later withdrawing the evidence by language which is clear and specific and from which the
jury cannot fail to understand exactly what is withdrawn from their
consideration. *Remus* v. *United States*, 291 Fed. 501 (1923), certiorari denied, 68 L. ed. 522 (1924).

a rule of great practical importance, yet, after all, it is only a rule of procedure, and therefore it is not to be applied as a hard and fast formula to every case, regardless of its special circumstances. We think, rather, that it is a rule to be used to secure the ends of justice under the circumstances of each case. . . A rule of practice must not be allowed for any technical reason to prevail over a constitutional right." And in the *Amos* case [17] decided at the same time, a petition for the return of evidence was held not presented too late when made after the jury was sworn but before any evidence was offered. In this case, none of the allegations in the petition were denied by the government and the examination and appropriate cross-examination in the regular course of the trial of the latter's own witnesses, called to make out its case, clearly showed the unconstitutional nature of the seizure.[18]

In *Agnello* v. *United States*,[19] where the defendant was excused from the obligation of petitioning before trial because he did not know of the seizure, the Court went on to lay down this rule:

Where, by uncontroverted facts, it appears that a search and seizure were made in violation of the Fourth Amendment, there is no reason why one whose rights have been so violated and who is sought to be incriminated by evidence so obtained, may not invoke protection of the Fifth Amendment immediately, and without any application for return of the thing seized.

But the fact is usually overlooked that notwithstanding these broad exceptions the collateral issue rule still stands. In the ordinary case, where the defendant has knowledge of the seizure and thus is afforded an opportunity of petitioning for the return of the evidence before the trial, the Court adheres to the rule and will not consider the matter merely upon the objection by the defendant in the course of the trial

---

[17] *Amos* v. *United States*, 255 U. S. 313, 65 L. ed. 654, 41 Sup. Ct. 266 (1921).

[18] "The facts essential to the disposition of the motion [to exclude the evidence] were not and could not be denied; they were literally thrust upon the attention of the court by the government itself. The petition should have been granted; but, it having been denied, the motion should have been sustained." *Ibid.*

[19] Cit. above.

to the admissibility of the evidence. This principle was re-affirmed and acted upon in the comparatively recent case of *Segurola* v. *United States.*[20]

So much for the procedural question as to how and when the alleged invasion of the constitutional right may be challenged. This is all-important, because if the Supreme Court had taken the extreme stand on the collateral issue rule adopted by many state courts, which prevents an application for the return of the evidence even before trial,[21] then the right as it affects the Federal Government under the Fourth Amendment would have lost all value to the party claiming its protection, as it has in those states which apply the extreme collateral issue rule. The Supreme Court has uniformly maintained, moreover, that the guilty are as equally entitled as the innocent to the protection of this right, which the Constitution provides *shall not be violated.*[22] This would seem to be necessarily so, since the violation always takes place before the guilt of the accused is established.

The Court also has indicated its opinion as to the value of the guaranty against unreasonable search and seizure and the perfecting of the right in certain cases by the Fifth Amendment in this strong language: " It would not be possible to add to the emphasis with which the framers of the Constitution and this Court have declared the importance to political liberty and to the welfare of our country of the due obser-

---

[20] 275 U. S. 106, 72 L. ed. 186, 48 Sup. Ct. 77 (1927). See also *McDaniel* v. *United States*, 294 Fed. 769 (1924).

If the correct argument is not advanced by the defendant for the return of the evidence and the lower court accordingly decides against him, that does not necessarily mean that he has lost his right to raise the correct objection upon appeal. In *Gambino* v. *United States*, counsel for the defendant did not take the correct position even before the Supreme Court, but the Court held that this would not interfere with the decision in his favor to reverse the conviction, when this conviction rested wholly upon the evidence which the Court concluded was obtained by invasion of the defendant's constitutional right. 275 U. S. 310, 72 L. ed. 293, 48 Sup. Ct. 137, 52 A. L. R. 1381 (1927).

[21] See *People* v. *Defore*, 242 N. Y. 13, 150 N. E. 585 (1926).

[22] *Boyd* v. *United States*, 116 U. S. 616, 31 L. ed. 80, 6 Sup. Ct. 524 (1886); *Go-Bart Importing Co.* v. *United States*, 282 U. S. 344, 75 L. ed. 374, 51 Sup. Ct. 153 (1931); *United States* v. *Lefkowitz*, 285 U. S. 452, 76 L. ed. 877, 52 Sup. Ct. 420 (1932).

vance of the rights guaranteed by these two Amendments."
The Fourth and Fifth Amendments are "indispensable to
the full enjoyment of personal security, personal liberty, and
private property; . . . they are to be regarded as of the very
essence of constitutional liberty; . . . the guaranty of them
is as important and as imperative as are the guaranties of
other fundamental rights of the individual citizen,—the right
to trial by jury, to the writ of habeas corpus, and to due
process of law." [23]

In accordance with this view and the view expressed in
the *Boyd* case, the Court has been careful in applying the
Fourth Amendment to prevent the circumvention of its provisions by the government. In the leading case of *Silverthorne Lumber Co.* v. *United States*,[24] federal officers, after
arresting defendants in their homes, went to their office, and
without the shadow of authority, made a clean sweep of all
books, papers, and records found there. Photographs and
copies of these were made, and an indictment framed thereon.
The lower court, upon application, ordered the return of the
original records because of the constitutional violation, but
retained the photographs and copies that had been made and
then, seeking to regain the originals by issuing a subpoena
duces tecum for their production, held the defendants in
contempt upon their refusal to comply. The Supreme Court,
in an opinion by Mr. Justice Holmes, ruled against the propriety of the procedure. "The essence of a provision forbidding the acquisition of evidence in a certain way," said
the Court, "is that not merely evidence so acquired shall
not be used before the court but that it should not be used
at all." To say that the government may seize papers unlawfully, which it now regrets, continued the opinion, but
may make copies and then use the very knowledge thus
gained by the unconstitutional act, which knowledge it would
otherwise not have had, again to call upon the owners for

[23] Mr. Justice Clarke, in *Gouled* v. *United* States, 255 U. S. 298, 65
L. ed. 647, 41 Sup. Ct. 261 (1921).

[24] 251 U. S. 385, 64 L. ed. 319, 40 Sup. Ct. 182, 24 A. L. R. 1426
(1920).

the originals, "would reduce the Fourth Amendment to a mere form of words." The indirection employed would avoid the general principle laid down in the *Weeks* case which prohibited using the evidence directly.[25]

Another question of procedure which may be disposed of at this point is that of appeal. When the trial court has refused a motion for the return of the evidence prior to the trial (and in many cases this will be determinative of the defendant's guilt); may the latter immediately appeal to a higher court on the alleged error in this ruling? Ordinarily, after indictment, when the prosecution is pending, the defendant cannot appeal directly because the ruling upon his motion is not a final judgment from which an appeal will lie. The court may change its mind during the trial and upon the usual objection to the admissibility of the evidence rule in favor of the defendant.[26] However, where the proceedings for the return of the evidence are *independent* of the principal case, as by a bill in equity, or upon motion by the owner who is a stranger to the case,[27] or where the motion is filed before indictment,[28] then an appeal will lie directly.[29]

The substantive provisions of the Amendment may now be examined more closely. To begin with, who are "the people" who may claim its protection? This term is not of course used in the sense of "nation" or even as embracing only citizens of the United States. An alien may claim the right on the same footing as any other.[30] A corporation,

---

[25] Chief Justice White and Mr. Justice Pitney dissented.

[26] *Cogen* v. *United States*, 278 U. S. 221, 73 L. ed. 275, 49 Sup. Ct. 118 (1929).

[27] *Go-Bart Importing Co.* v. *United States*, cit. above.

[28] *Ibid.*

[29] *Cogen* v. *United States*, cit. above.

[30] *Fong Yue Ting* v. *United States*, 149 U. S. 698, 37 L. ed. 905, 13 Sup. Ct. 1016 (1892) ; *United States* ex rel. *Bilokumsky* v. *Tod*, 263 U. S. 149, 68 L. ed. 221, 44 Sup. Ct. 54 (1923).
In the *Fong Yue Ting* case, the Court held, however, that with regard to *deportation* proceedings such guaranties as the Fourth Amendment had no application since deportation is not a criminal proceeding. But it seems that at the present time this ruling is no longer adhered to. In the more recent *Bilokumsky* case, the Court said, *obiter dictum*, that it may be assumed that evidence obtained by an illegal search and seizure cannot be made the basis of a find-

although it is not a natural person and although it has been held not to be such a " person " as to come within the terms of the closely related self-incrimination clause of the Fifth Amendment, is also entitled to its benefits.[31]

It must not be understood that because of the mere fact that evidence has been seized by means of an unconstitutional search or seizure a defendant, *ipso facto,* has the right to demand its suppression. The defendant cannot complain where it is not he who has been the subject of the unreasonable search. In such case, he cannot request the return of the property, since it does not belong to him, and no rights of *his* under the Fourth Amendment have been violated.[32] In addition, he cannot maintain that by the seizure and use in evidence of someone else's papers or other property the government has compelled *him* to incriminate *himself*. In similar manner, an officer of a corporation is not in a position to refuse to surrender the records of the corporation on the ground that he will thereby incriminate himself.[33]

---

ing in a deportation case. A lower federal court has made this very decision, but without even noticing the *Fong Yue Ting* case. And see the principles laid down by the Department of Labor as applicable to deportation cases in the article by Fraenkel, *Harvard Law Review,* XXXIV, 361, 376-377.

[31] *Hale* v. *Henkel,* 201 U. S. 43, 50 L. ed. 652, 26 Sup. Ct. 370 (1906); *Consolidated Rendering Co.* v. *Vermont,* 207 U. S. 541, 52 L. ed. 327, 28 Sup. Ct. 178 (1908).

Upon the more academic question of whether a slave, before the Civil War, could have insisted upon the right, it seems clear that he could, upon the definite contrast between the choice of the term " people," as opposed to " freemen," to whom the right had been limited in the provisions for a bill of rights recommended by several of the states to the First Congress. See page 95 n., above.

[32] *Remus* v. *United States,* 291 Fed. 501 (1923), certiorari denied, 68 L. ed. 522 (1924).

[33] *Wilson* v. *United States,* 221 U. S. 361, 55 L. ed. 771, 31 Sup. Ct. 538, Ann. Cas. 1912D 508 (1911); *Wheeler* v. *United States,* 226 U. S. 478, 57 L. ed. 309, 33 Sup. Ct. 158 (1912).

The privileges guaranteed may be waived by a party who is entitled to assert them. Where a warrant is irregular for some reason, but no objection is made until after trial, the irregularity is considered waived. *Albrecht* v. *United States,* 273 U. S. 1, 71 L. ed. 505, 47 Sup. Ct. 250 (1926).

Where prohibition agents were let into defendant's house after demanding entrance, it has been held that this was no waiver of the defendant's constitutional right, because of the implied coercion by demanding admission as officers of the government. *Amos* v. *United States,* 255 U. S. 313, 65 L. ed., 654, 41 Sup. Ct. 266 (1921).

Before we approach the problem as to what constitutes an *unreasonable* search and seizure, we might consider the cases wherein the question was raised as to whether, indeed, the acts of the officials involved constituted a search and seizure at all. In *Olmstead* v. *United States*,[34] popularly known as the " Wire-Tapping Case," prohibition agents tapped the telephone wires leading to the defendants' office and their homes without trespassing upon any part of the premises belonging to them. The Court held, in an opinion by Chief Justice Taft, that to amount to a search and seizure within the Fourth Amendment of " persons, houses, papers, and effects " there must be an official search and seizure of the person, or a search of his papers or other *tangible* effects, or an actual physical invasion of his house for the purpose of making a seizure. The *Gouled* case which held that a secret taking of papers from the defendant's house or office without force constituted a search and seizure, because the security and privacy of those places were as much invaded and as much against the will of the owner whether accomplished by force or by fraud and stealth, carried the law, the Court said, to the extreme limit and was not to be enlarged. In that case at least there was an actual entry and the seizure of something *tangible,* whereas here it was only voluntary conversations that were secretly overheard.

Four justices dissented from the majority opinion. Mr. Justice Brandeis presented a powerful argument in the principal dissent wherein he contended, among other things, that the privacy of the individual was just as much invaded by wire-tapping. as in the other cases held to be searches and seizures. Since the *powers* of the government can be extended to new objects—not contemplated by the framers of the Constitution because unknown to them—objects that have been brought out by modern invention and conditions, he argued that the *limitations* upon the government should receive a corresponding liberal construction to bring them in line according to their spirit with present conditions.[35]

---

[34] 277 U. S. 438, 72 L. ed. 944, 48 Sup. Ct. 564 (1928).
[35] A statute of the state that made wire-tapping a criminal offense also played an important part in the dissenting opinion.

In the *Jackson* case, which has already been mentioned as one of the earlier cases, the Court held that opening a sealed letter in the mails was a search and seizure which required a warrant to make it legal.[36] This holding is distinguishable from the *Olmstead* case, because in the earlier case an actual seizure of tangible property had taken place. The ruling also in the *Boyd* case and in the decisions involving the production of papers in response to a subpoena *duces tecum,* that this amounts to a search and seizure even though there is no physical invasion of the dwelling, may be distinguished on the ground that the government in such cases forces the delivery into its hands of *tangible* evidence by another form of coercion.[37]

On the other hand, it has been held that mere interrogation under oath by a government official of one lawfully in confinement is not a search and seizure.[38] So also, where prohibition agents pursued the defendant over a field and the latter dropped a jug and a bottle, the Court held that there was no seizure in the sense of the law when the officers examined the contents of the jug and bottle after they had been abandoned.[39] And in another case,[40] where certain articles which the defendant had produced *voluntarily* in a patent case in which he was interested, and which had been impounded to perpetuate the evidence in the custody of the clerk of the court, were used before the grand jury in order to obtain an indictment against him, it was held that there was no violation of either the Fourth or Fifth Amendments,

---

[36] 96 U. S. 727, 24 L. ed. 877 (1877). In England, the mail may apparently be opened at will by the proper officials. In other respects the restrictions upon search and seizure are probably more strict than in this country. See Wood, *West Virginia Law Quarterly,* XXXIV, 139, 143, 154.

[37] *Hale* v. *Henkel,* 201 U. S. 43, 50 L. ed. 652, 26 Sup. Ct. 370 (1906).

[38] *United States* ex rel. *Bilokumsky* v. *Tod,* 263 U. S. 149, 68 L. ed. 221, 44 Sup. Ct. 263 (1923). See also *Re Chapman,* 166 U. S. 661, 41 L. ed. 1154, 17 Sup. Ct. 677 (1896).

[39] *Hester* v. *United States,* 265 U. S. 57, 68 L. ed. 898, 44 Sup. Ct. 445 (1924).

[40] *Perlman* v. *United States,* 247 U. S. 7, 62 L. ed. 950, 38 Sup. Ct. 417 (1917).

since there had been no invasion of the defendant's privacy nor a taking from his possession.[41]

The Amendment provides that if there is to be a search and seizure, it must be a reasonable one.[42] The only absolute standard that is set is as to the essentials of a warrant when such is necessary, as it is in most cases. The purpose of the latter part of the Amendment of course is to safeguard against the general warrant and it does this in two ways: first, by prescribing the requirement of probable cause, necessarily peculiar to each case; and second, by making requisite the description of the particular place to be searched, the persons to be apprehended, and the objects to be seized. These requirements limit the scope of each warrant; they take the decision as to what may and what may not be done out of the hands of the officer who is to execute the warrant, and place it with the more trustworthy and sober judgment of a judicial officer. It is for the latter to pass upon the merits of the allegations and, on the basis of evidence having behind it the responsibility of an oath, to decide whether there is reasonable justification for this exceptional proceeding in invasion of the individual's privacy, and thus to determine what particular actions are justified on the basis of this showing. There is no temptation for the ministerial officer to exceed the authority which the magistrate decides to give him, for he not only thereby subjects himself to civil and criminal liability but gains no advantage over the accused and merely wastes his effort.

In addition to the constitutional standard and in furtherance thereof, Congress has provided certain regulations and limitations which must be followed. According to statute, search warrants in federal cases may be issued by a district judge, by a judge of a state or territorial court of record, or

---

[41] In *Flint* v. *Stone Tracy Co.*, 220 U. S. 107, 55 L. ed. 389, 31 Sup. Ct. 342 (1910), the Court held that the feature of the corporation tax law which made returns available to public inspection did not violate the principle of the Fourth Amendment.

[42] " There is no formula for the determination of reasonableness. Each case is to be decided on its own facts and circumstances." *Go-Bart Importing Co.* v. *United States*, 282 U. S. 344, 357, 75 L. ed. 374, 51 Sup. Ct. 153 (1931).

by a United States commissioner,[43] and directed to any civil officer of the United States authorized to enforce its laws or to any other person authorized by the President.[44] Warrants may be issued only for the search of property *used as a means* of committing a felony, for stolen or embezzled goods, or property or papers used to violate the espionage laws.[45] Before issuing a warrant the judge or commissioner must examine the complainant and any other witnesses under oath, require their affidavits, and have their depositions taken down in writing and signed by them.[46] If he is then satisfied that the grounds of the application exist or that there is probable cause to believe their existence, he must issue the warrant and sign it in his official capacity, stating the particular grounds or probable cause for the warrant and the names of those persons whose affidavits have been taken in support of it.[47] The statute repeats in almost so many words the constitutional requirement that the warrant must specify the places to be searched and the persons or property to be seized.[48]

The warrant may be executed, in addition, only by the officer to whom it is directed and such others as he may call to assist him in the execution of his duty.[49] Moreover, it is only if he is refused admittance after he has given notice of

---

[43] 18 U. S. C. A., sec. 611.

[44] *Ibid.*, sec. 616. In *Steele* v. *United States*, 267 U. S. 505, 69 L. ed. 761, 45 Sup. Ct. 417 (1925), it was settled that a prohibition agent was an officer of the United States to whom a warrant may be issued. See also *Dumbra* v. *United States*, 268 U. S. 435, 69 L. ed. 1032, 45 Sup. Ct. 546 (1925).

[45] 18 U. S. C. A., sec. 612. See *Veeder* v. *United States*, 252 Fed. 414 (1918), certiorari denied, 246 U. S. 675 (1918); *Gouled* v. *United States*, 255 U. S. 298, 65 L. ed. 647, 41 Sup. Ct. 261 (1921); *Schenck* v. *United States*, 249 U. S. 47, 63 L. ed. 470, 39 Sup. Ct. 247 (1919).

[46] 18 U. S. C. A., sec. 614.

[47] *Ibid.*, secs. 615, 616.

[48] *Ibid.*, sec. 613.

[49] *Ibid.*, sec. 617. In *Go-Bart Importing Co.* v. *United States*, 282 U. S. 344, 75 L. ed. 374, 51 Sup. Ct. 153 (1931), a warrant directed to a marshal and his deputies which had been issued upon the complaint of a prohibition agent was held to authorize no one but those designated in the warrant, and a search thereunder by the prohibition agent was accordingly held invalid.

his authority and purpose that he may break into the place specified in the warrant.[50] And the warrant must limit the time of search to the daytime unless the affidavits are positive that the property is in the place to be searched.[51]

To be a reasonable search and seizure, the warrant of course cannot be good indefinitely in the hands of the officer. Congress has set the time for the return of the warrant at ten days and if it is not executed within that time it becomes void.[52] When he seizes property, the officer must give a copy of the warrant to the person from whom he has taken the property, together with a detailed receipt of what he has seized. If no one is present, he must leave an inventory.[53] A copy of this inventory under the officer's oath must be returned with the warrant to the issuing magistrate, and the property must also be brought before the latter, who orders it retained in the custody of the officer or otherwise disposed of according to law.[54] But if it then or later appears that the property is not the same as that described in the warrant or that there was no probable cause for believing

---

[50] 18 U. S. C. A., sec. 618.   [51] *Ibid.*, sec. 620.

[52] Ibid., sec. 621. In a recent case the facts were that a prohibition agent procured a search warrant upon an affidavit that beer was sold to him in a hotel. He did not execute the warrant in the ten days allowed, so he sent it back to the commissioner who had issued it and the latter redated it. The Court held, in an opinion by Chief Justice Hughes, that the warrant could not be revived by redating it. The provision that the warrant is void if not executed within ten days, said the Court, must be read in the light of the requirement that probable cause must appear to the satisfaction of the magistrate before he may issue it. This marks the permitted duration of the proceedings. The proof must have an appropriate relationship to the application for a new warrant, which is really a new proceeding, and must speak as of the time of that warrant. The new warrant must rest upon a proper finding that probable cause *then* exists. *Sgro* v. *United States*, 287 U. S. 206, 77 L. ed. 260, 52 Sup. Ct. 138 (1932).

Justices Stone and Cardozo dissented on the ground that as a matter of fact the second warrant was sufficiently supported by the facts set forth in the first affidavit. It is interesting to note that since the latter justice has been on the Supreme Bench he has twice dissented in favor of the government. It is perhaps to be remembered that Mr. Justice Cardozo, while on the New York Court of Appeals, was one of the leading exponents of the extreme collateral issue doctrine. See *People* v. *Defore*, 242 N. Y. 13, 150 N. E. 585 (1926).

[53] 18 U. S. C. A., sec. 622.   [54] *Ibid.*, sec. 623.

the existence of the grounds upon which it was issued, then the magistrate must order its return to its owner.[55]

The statute further provides penalties for the abuse of the process. Perjury or subornation of perjury in procuring a warrant is subject to heavy fine and imprisonment.[56] Any person who maliciously and without probable cause obtains the issuance of a warrant is also subject to fine and imprisonment and any officer who in executing a search warrant " willfully exceeds his authority, or exercises it with unnecessary severity," may be fined $1,000 and imprisoned for one year.[57]

These are the principal provisions of the federal statutory law with regard to the issuance of warrants. But since a warrant is not necessary in every case of search and seizure, the question may now be taken up as to when a warrant is necessary to validate the acts of the officer and when not.

Primarily, the answer to this question is dependent upon two major considerations. The first is concerned with the degree in which the acts of the officer will invade the privacy of people, the second with the practicability of being able to get a warrant in time to accomplish its purpose.[58] Now, with regard to the dwelling house, the traditions of time imme-

---

[55] *Ibid.*, sec. 624.

[56] *Ibid.*, sec. 629.

[57] *Ibid.*, secs. 630-631.

In *Maguire* v. *United States*, 273 U. S. 95, 71 L. ed. 556, 47 Sup. Ct. 259 (1927), prohibition agents had entered defendant's premises under a valid search warrant but had unlawfully destroyed all the liquor found, except a small amount to be used as evidence. The defendant contended that this illegal execution of the warrant reverted back, by application of the doctrine of trespass *ab initio*, to vitiate the whole proceeding. The Court held, however, that this doctrine had no application and that the legal seizure of the evidential liquor under the valid warrant was distinct from the illegal destruction of the rest.

Despite the numerous illegal searches and seizures, however, that have taken place, it seems that this provision of the act has never been enforced. See Thomas E. Atkinson, " Admissibility of Evidence through Unreasonable Searches and Seizures," *Columbia Law Review*, 1925, XXV, 11, and " Prohibition and the Doctrine of the Weeks Case," *Michigan Law Review*, 1925, XXIII, 748, by the same writer. The *United States Code Annotated* contains no annotations under this section.

[58] See the excellent analysis by Wood, in *West Virginia Law Quarterly*, XXXIV, 1, 137.

morial still control in holding its privacy to be most inviolable. At the same time, there is always the opportunity to seek the authority of a warrant without fear that the place of search will remove itself. The only circumstance which allows entry and search of a dwelling without a warrant is that in which the officer witnesses the commission of an offense inside the house and therefore has the right to enter for the purpose of making the arrest. Then, on the basis of the old common law rule which permits search when it is incidental to a lawful arrest, he may search the persons of those apprehended and the immediate premises for such things connected with the crime as its fruits, or the means by which it was committed, or weapons and other things with which to effect an escape from custody. Searches of dwellings without a valid warrant are otherwise unlawful, notwithstanding facts unquestionably showing probable cause.[59] Upon the same considerations, this rule has been held to apply to offices also.[60] And the Court has recently held in one case that prohibition officers could not enter and search even a garage for liquor, especially where there was opportunity to secure a warrant for that purpose.[61] But a warrant is not necessary to enter upon someone's field, even though

---

[59] *Agnello* v. *United States*, 269 U. S. 20, 70 L. ed. 145, 46 Sup. Ct. 4, 51 A. L. R. 409 (1925).

Under the Prohibition Act, a dwelling which was used wholly as such and not in part for some business purpose, could not be searched even with a warrant, unless there was evidence of the unlawful *sale* of liquor on the premises (41 Stat. L. 305, 315). In the case of a dwelling, then, where the evidence pointed only to the unlawful *manufacture* of liquor a search warrant could not be procured, and the Supreme Court held that the unlawful *sale* of liquor could not be inferred solely from evidence of manufacture on a large scale, this so as not to nullify the distinction which Congress had clearly laid down. *Grau* v. *United States*, 287 U. S. 124, 77 L. ed. 212, 53 Sup. Ct. 38 (1932).

In *Steele* v. *United States*, 267 U. S. 498, 69 L. ed. 757, 45 Sup. Ct. 414 (1925), it was held that the fact that an employee of the defendant cooked and slept in one of the rooms did not give the building the character of a private dwelling.

[60] *Silverthorne Lumber Co.* v. *United States*, 251 U. S. 385, 64 L. ed. 319, 40 Sup. Ct. 182, 24 A. L. R. 1426 (1920); *Go-Bart Importing Co.* v. *United States*, 282 U. S. 344, 75 L. ed., 374, 51 Sup. Ct. 153 (1931).

[61] *Taylor* v. *United States*, 286 U. S. 1, 76 L. ed. 951, 52 Sup. Ct. 466 (1932).

such would constitute a trespass on the part of the officer. The protection of the Fourth Amendment to the people in their " persons, houses, papers, and effects " does not extend to the open fields, the Court has said, the distinction between the latter and the house being as old as the common law.[62]

In the case of movable vehicles, however, the factor of practicability becomes the predominant consideration. Also it is true that the privacy of the individual is much less invaded in such a case than in the case of a dwelling or other building. In the searching of automobiles, then, where as a practical matter it would be impossible to procure a warrant in time to effect a search, the same rule applies as has always held in the case of vessels; namely, that no warrant but only the existence of probable cause is necessary to constitute the search a reasonable one.[63] That the Fourth Amendment did not contemplate a warrant in such an instance is rendered more certain by the fact that the First Congress, which itself framed the Amendment, drew a distinction in its duty collection statute between the necessity for a warrant where goods subject to forfeiture for non-payment of customs were suspected of being concealed in a building, and where like goods in course of transportation were concealed in a vessel and could thereby readily be put out of the reach of a search warrant.[64] The doctrine which permits search in the case of movable vehicles, accordingly, is based upon the holding that if there is probable cause to believe that an offense is being committed, the search is not an unreasonable one within the meaning of the Amendment. Since the rule is entirely independent of that one which permits the search of a dwelling without a warrant when incidental

---

[62] *Hester* v. *United States*, 265 U. S. 57, 68 L. ed. 898, 44 Sup. Ct. 445 (1924).

[63] *Carroll* v. *United States*, 267 U. S. 132, 69 L. ed. 543, 45 Sup. Ct. 280, 39 A. L. R. 790 (1925); *Husty* v. *United States*, 282 U. S. 694, 75 L. ed. 629, 51 Sup. Ct. 240, 74 A. L. R. 1407 (1931). See also *United States* v. *Lee*, 274 U. S. 640, 71 L. ed. 1202, 47 Sup. Ct. 746 (1927); *Maul* v. *United States*, 274 U. S. 501, 71 L. ed. 1171, 47 Sup. Ct. 735 (1927).

[64] 1 Stat. L. 145, 170. See also *ibid.*, pp. 305, 315, 627, 677, 678.

to a lawful arrest, no prior arrest or, indeed, no arrest at all has to be made for the search to be valid.[65]

In an appropriate case, however, where the principal basis for this exception as to movable vehicles does not apply, e. g., where the automobile for some reason will not be able to be moved or where a vessel, let us say, is firmly beached, and there consequently is time to respect the safeguard of a warrant, it is reasonable to suppose that upon the *ratio decidendi* of the automobile cases a warrant might be held necessary in such an instance. In the *Husty* case,[66] where the automobile in question had been parked, the objection was made that the search was unreasonable because there had been sufficient time to get a warrant. The answer given by the Court was not simply that a warrant was not essential for the search of an automobile, but that in the particular case the officer could not know when the defendant was going to move the automobile and consequently whether there was time or not to get a warrant.[67]

Closely related to the question of search without a warrant is that of search incidental to arrest. In the *Agnello* case,[68] where government agents watching at a window saw the defendants selling narcotics, the entry of the house and subsequent search without a warrant were justified as incidental to the lawful arrest. The search of course could not have been incidental if it had preceded and resulted in the arrest.[69]

Now, after the arrest, the authority of the officers extends

---

[65] See *Carroll* v. *United States*, cit. above, and *Husty* v. *United States*, cit. above.

[66] *Ibid.*

[67] Compare also the consideration of this factor of practicability in *Taylor* v. *United States*, 286 U. S. 1, 76 L. ed. 951, 52 Sup. Ct. 466 (1932).

[68] *Agnello* v. *United States*, 269 U. S. 20, 70 L. ed. 145, 46 Sup. Ct. 4, 51 A. L. R. 409 (1925).

[69] *Taylor* v. *United States*, cit. above. In this case, the officers smelled the odor of whiskey near the garage and, looking in, saw many boxes and other materials indicative of the violation of the Volstead Act. But they saw no one inside committing the offense. The entering and search were held illegal without a warrant. The defendant was arrested after the search when he came out of the house to see what was going on, but this arrest was held not to validate the act of the officers.

to articles in the immediate control of the one arrested, where-
ever found in the premises used for the unlawful purpose,[70]
but to these premises only, so that an arrest does not justify,
as incidental thereto, the search of the house where the person arrested lives, when the arrest has taken place elsewhere.[71]   Moreover, there is no such thing as search incidental to the execution of a search warrant. The Court expressly overruled this bold contention made by the government in one case which would have directly avoided the very
particularity required by the Constitution itself to be observed in the warrant.[72] However, in the same case, *Marron*
v. *United States*,[73] where the prohibition agents had a warrant to search for intoxicating liquor and, once lawfully inside, arrested the bartender in the act of selling liquor, there
was upheld as *incidental to the arrest* the seizure of a ledger
and certain bills not mentioned in the warrant.

The implications of the *Marron* case, which seemed to go
far toward permitting a general search for unspecified articles, just so the officer could manage to effect a valid arrest
after he had lawfully entered under a warrant,[74] have been
narrowed to a considerable extent in an opinion recently
handed down, in which the Court experienced some difficulty
in distinguishing the *Marron* case both upon this point and

---

[70] *Marron* v. *United States*, 275 U. S. 192, 72 L. ed. 231, 48 Sup.
Ct. 74 (1927).
[71] *Weeks* v. *United States*, 232 U. S. 383. 58 L. ed. 652, 34 Sup.
Ct. 341, L. R. A. 1915B 834, Ann. Cas. 1915C 1117 (1914); *Silverthorne Lumber Co.* v. *United States*, 251 U. S. 385, 64 L. ed. 319, 40
Sup. Ct. 182, 24 A. L. R. 1426 (1920); *Agnello* v. *United States*,
cit. above.
[72] Cf. the language used by the Court in the *Adams* case as regards
evidence, seized under a search warrant, other than that specified in
the warrant. 192 U. S. 585, 48 L. ed. 575, 24 Sup. Ct. 372 (1903).
Cf. also the *Weeks* case (cit. above), in which the Court reiterated
that one of the grounds upon which the *Adams* case rested was
incidental seizure made in the execution of a legal search warrant.
[73] Cit. above.
[74] The whole doctrine of search incidental to arrest runs counter
in a measure to the particularity required by the Fourth Amendment, as witness the result reached in the *Marron* case. See *Wise* v.
Mills, 185 Fed. 318 (1911); Fraenkel, *Harvard Law Review*,
XXXIV, 361, notes 46, 115, 127.

upon another which will be taken up later. In this case,[75] federal officers with a valid *warrant of arrest* entered defendants' office and, effecting the arrests, started a general exploratory search of the room, searching in desks, cabinets, and waste baskets for incriminating evidence and taking away certain papers which the government later attempted to use against the defendants. Here, then, as in the *Marron* case, there was a *valid arrest* and a search for and seizure of evidence on the premises, which evidence was in the immediate control of those legally arrested. But the Court held that the evidence was obtained by means of an unreasonable search and seizure. The *Marron* case was distinguished on the ground that the arrest was made for a crime which was being committed in the presence of the officers and on the ground that the ledger and bills, which the Court said were in plain view in the earlier case, were picked up without any search being made for them. In this case, on the other hand, there was only a *warrant of arrest* to be executed by the officers, no crime was being committed in their presence, and a real and independent search was made for the incriminating evidence.[76]

The rule of search of premises incidental to arrest, accordingly, would now seem to apply not to lawful arrest in general, but only to those instances where the arrest takes place because the defendant has committed a crime in the presence of the officer.[77] The search in such a case must be limited to the person of the offender and to that property in his immediate control on the premises, but in the latter instance the property must be in plain view, or in such a place that the

---

[75] *United States* v. *Lefkowitz*, 285 U. S. 452, 76 L. ed. 877, 52 Sup. Ct. 420 (1932).

[76] Cf. *Adams* v. *New York*, cit. above.

By an independent search the Court does not mean, it would seem, that actual force necessarily has to be employed, since the facts in the *Lefkowitz* case showed that the desks and cabinets were not locked and no breaking was necessary.

[77] In the case of any lawful arrest, however, it would still be permissible to search the persons of those arrested. See the *Lefkowitz* case (cit. above), affirming the opinion of the lower court reported in 52 Fed.(2d) 52 (1931). See also *Go-Bart Importing Co.* v. *United States*, 282 U. S. 344, 75 L. ed. 374, 51 Sup. Ct. 153 (1931).

officer can perceive it without any special search and secure it without any threat of force or rummaging of the place.[78]

The decisions of the Supreme Court with respect to the features of the warrant itself, when one is necessary, may now be considered. First and most important, there is the element of probable cause. Involved in this requirement are two factors: first, whether the facts charged are sufficient to constitute an offense against the law; and second, whether the facts presented justify a reasonable belief that the offense was actually committed, that it was the accused who committed it and, if it is a search warrant, that the property is in the place sought to be searched. If the complaint does not state a good legal cause, the warrant is invalid on its face and the officer derives no authority from it.[79] But if the warrant states an offense sufficiently and evidence is seized under such a valid warrant, the evidence thus legally seized may be used against the defendant in a prosecution for a different offense.[80]

The probable cause required in a warrant by the Constitution must be proved by competent legal testimony, just as in the trial of a case.[81] It might be indicated at this point, although the matter does not seem to have struck the attention of writers, that herein lies a distinct difference between the requisite probable cause of a warrant and that which is necessary to search a movable vehicle without a warrant. This difference is as to the quality of the evidence which may go to prove the probable cause, and is sanctioned by the same exigency upon which is based the exception itself that per-

---

[78] See the *Go-Bart* case (*ibid.*), where the Court mentioned that the records seized in the *Marron* case as incidental to the arrest were all visible and accessible and in the offender's immediate custody, and that there was no threat of force, general search, or rummaging. Incidentally, the ledger seized in the *Marron* case was found in a closet while the officers were searching for the liquor specified in their warrant.

[79] *Ex parte Burford*, 3 Cr. 448, 2 L. ed. 495 (1806); *Go-Bart Importing Co.* v. *United States*, cit. above.

[80] *Gouled* v. *United States*, 255 U. S. 298, 65 L. ed. 647, 41 Sup. Ct. 261 (1921).

[81] *Grau* v. *United States*, 287 U. S. 124, 77 L. ed. 212, 53 Sup. Ct. 38 (1932).

mits search of vehicles without a warrant. In order to constitute probable cause for the search of an automobile, the evidence which may be considered by the officer does not have to be of a legally competent nature and he may base his conclusion upon grounds which a magistrate in determining the same question before issuing a warrant could not take into consideration.[82] Thus, mere hearsay may be one of the elements considered in such a case by an officer [83] and the facts need not bear such a proximate relationship in point of time to the question of probable cause as in warrant proceedings.[84]

The Court has held, departing slightly from common law traditions, that a preliminary finding of probable cause is only a quasi-judicial act, one which is not such that it must necessarily be passed upon by a strictly judicial officer or tribunal.[85] In *Ocampo* v. *United States*,[86] accordingly, an act of the Philippine legislature was held valid which placed the function in the hands of the prosecuting attorney.

A warrant which merely states the conclusion that the affiant has good reason to believe and does believe that the defendant is in illegal possession of intoxicating liquor is clearly defective.[87] The affiant must take oath to the *facts* and *circumstances* that go to support a conclusion of probable cause and not merely to his belief that probable cause exists, since it is for the magistrate who issues the warrant to draw the necessary legal conclusion.[88] In point of time also, as has been mentioned before, the facts and circumstances to be considered in determining probable cause must have an ap-

---

[82] *Husty* v. *United States*, 282 U. S. 694, 75 L. ed. 629, 51 Sup. Ct. 240, 74 A. L. R. 1407 (1931).

[83] *Ibid.*

[84] Compare *Sgro* v. *United States*, 287 U. S. 206, 77 L. ed. 260, 53 Sup. Ct. 138 (1932) with *Carroll* v. *United States*, 267 U. S. 132, 69 L. ed. 543, 45 Sup. Ct. 280, 39 A. L. R. 790 (1925).

[85] Compare Hale, *Pleas of the Crown*, II, 79, 150, discussed in chap. i, above.

[86] 234 U. S. 91, 58 L. ed. 1231, 34 Sup. Ct. 712 (1914).

[87] *Nathanson* v. *United States*, 290 U. S. 41, 78 L. ed. 159, 54 Sup. Ct. 11 (1933); *Byars* v. *United States*, 273 U. S. 28, 71 L. ed. 520, 47 Sup. Ct. 248 (1927). See also *Grau* v. *United States*, cit. above.

[88] *Veeder* v. *United States*, 252 Fed. 414 (1918), certiorari denied, 246 U. S. 675 (1918).

propriate relationship to the issuance of the warrant and must speak as of that time.[89] At the trial of a case, if the point is properly raised whether there was probable cause to support the search and seizure, the question, it has been held, is one of law and fact to be decided by the court and not by the jury.[90]

As to the affidavit, the presumption prevails that a magistrate administered the requisite oaths.[91] A federal warrant contemplates an oath taken before an official authorized to administer oaths in federal criminal proceedings, so that an arrest by warrant under authority of a federal court upon an affidavit verified before a notary public has been held to violate the Fourth Amendment, as made without proper verification.[92] But the government may correct such a defect in the warrant unless the defendant has objected to the validity of the warrant before the irregularity has been cured by the prosecuting authorities. Therefore the defendant loses his right to object when his motion to quash the warrant is not made until after the government has filed proper affidavits.

In *McGrain* v. *Daugherty*,[93] decided in 1927, the Court held that a warrant of arrest issued on report of a Senate committee, acting upon its own knowledge without oath, is not invalid under the provision of the Fourth Amendment that no warrant shall issue but upon probable cause, sup-

---

[89] *Sgro* v. *United States*, cit. above.

[90] *Steele* v. *United States*, 267 U. S. 498, 505, 69 L. ed. 757, 761, 45 Sup. Ct. 414, 417 (1925). For other cases decided by the Court that involved determinations of whether probable cause did or did not exist, see *Carroll* v. *United States*, 267 U. S. 132, 69 L. ed, 543, 45 Sup. Ct. 280, 39 A. L. R. 790 (1925); *Dumbra* v. *United States*, 268 U. S. 435, 69 L. ed. 1032, 45 Sup. Ct. 546 (1925); *Gambino* v. *United States*, 275 U. S. 310, 72 L. ed. 293, 48 Sup. Ct. 137, 52 A. L. R. 1381 (1927); *Husty* v. *United States*, 282 U. S. 694, 75 L. ed. 629, 51 Sup. Ct. 240, 74 A. L. R. 1407 (1931); *Grau* v. *United States*, cit. above. The *Carroll*, *Gambino*, and *Husty* cases were automobile cases of search without warrant. The facts of the *Gambino* case, however, are not available since neither the Supreme Court nor the lower courts stated them.

[91] *Ex parte Bollman and Swartwout*, 4 Cr. 75, 2 L. ed. 554 (1807).

[92] *Albrecht* v. *United States*, 273 U. S. 1, 71 L. ed. 505, 47 Sup. Ct. 250 (1926).

[93] 273 U. S. 135, 71 L. ed. 580, 47 Sup. Ct. 319, 50 A. L. R. 1 (1927).

ported by oath or affirmation, since the members of the committee were acting under their oaths of office as senators.
The Court supported this rather strained construction of the
Amendment with the statement that the principle was also
recognized in judicial proceedings in the issuance of contempt warrants and warrants issued at the instance of a
grand jury, and that the practice in the Senate was an old
established one.

The Amendment requires that the place to be searched
should be stated specifically. The description of the place
must be such, therefore, that the officer with the warrant may
with reasonable effort ascertain and identify the premises
intended. Applying this principle in *Steele* v. *United
States*,[94] the Court held that where two buildings were joined,
with a garage entrance in the middle over which was a sign
" Truck Service, No. 609 and 611," and one elevator led to
both sides, a warrant issued to search No. 611 of that street,
described as a garage and for business purposes, indicated the
whole building as the place intended and authorized search
throughout the whole premises.

With regard to the person, the Supreme Court has insisted
upon a great degree of particularity. In *West* v. *Cabell*,[95] a
United States marshal intended to arrest as suspected of a
certain crime one Vandy M. West, but procured a warrant
authorizing the arrest of James West, with no further description of the person. The arrest under this warrant of Vandy
M. West, the man actually wanted, who had never been known
by any other name, was held to be unlawful by the Court,
which ruled that the requirement that the party must be
named or *described* had to be strictly adhered to and that
the private intention of the magistrate and officer was no
substitute for the constitutional requirement.[96]

The property to be seized must be stipulated in the warrant and none other but that described therein may be taken.

---

[94] Cit. above.

[95] 153 U. S. 78, 38 L. ed. 643, 14 Sup. Ct. 752 (1893).

[96] This is the only case that has ever come before the Supreme
Court involving a civil suit for damages for an illegal seizure. This
was a suit on the marshal's bond.

It has been shown, however, how property not specified in any warrant may be seized as incidental to a lawful arrest for an offense being committed in the presence of the officer.

But with or without a warrant, specified or unspecified, there is certain property which *may not be searched for and seized at all.* It was early laid down in the *Boyd* case [97] that only that class of property to which the government is otherwise entitled or to which its possessor is not entitled, as stolen goods, counterfeit money, implements used to commit a crime, etc., is seizable under a search warrant, whereas a person's private books and papers cannot be so taken, in order merely to get information from them to be used in evidence against him.[98] In other words, the Court there drew a distinction between "contraband" property and property of merely "evidential" value.[99]

This distinction has been further developed by later cases, especially the important case of *Gouled* v. *United States.*[100] In that case, a number of contracts and bills belonging to defendants, who were suspected of conspiring to defraud the government through the agency of certain clothing contracts, were seized under search warrants. The Court held that the seizure of these papers was a violation of the Fourth Amendment. At common law and as a result of the *Boyd* and *Weeks* cases, said the Court in an opinion by Mr. Justice Clarke, search warrants cannot be employed to get into a house or office to search for evidence, merely for the purpose of using it against the accused in a trial. Warrants are allowed only where the primary right to such a search and seizure is in the interest which the public or complainant

---

[97] 116 U. S. 616, 29 L. ed. 746, 6 Sup. Ct. 524 (1886). See the discussion of this case earlier in the chapter.

[98] Compare the procedure for the *compulsory* production of documentary evidence by subpoena *duces tecum.*

[99] In the case of any lawful arrest, however, as pointed out above, it is permissible to search the person of the one who is arrested and in such an instance the cases seem to hold that even papers of merely evidential value may be legally seized and introduced in evidence. See the *Lefkowitz* case, 285 U. S. 452, 76 L. ed. 877, 52 Sup. Ct. 420 (1932), and also the opinion of the lower court in that case, 52 Fed.(2d) 52 (1913); *Go-Bart Importing Co.* v. *United States*, 282 U. S. 344, 75 L. ed. 374, 51 Sup. Ct. 153 (1931).

[100] 255 U. S. 298, 65 L. ed. 647, 41 Sup. Ct. 261 (1921).

may have in the property seized. This does not mean, the Court hastened to add, that all papers are immune from search and seizure. If these papers should fall within the scope of the principles permitting the seizure of other property, they may also be taken under a warrant. Stolen or forged papers, for example, or lottery tickets under a statute prohibiting their possession with intent to sell, are seizable. So also, contracts that are used as instruments to perpetrate frauds upon the government would give the public an interest in their seizure to prevent further frauds.

The government had here seized an unexecuted contract, an attorney's bill for services, and one executed contract. As to the first two, the Court could not see the interest the government might have in them to prevent injury to the public, other than merely to use them in evidence against the defendant. The executed contract, on the other hand, might very easily come within the principle by which seizure would be permitted, said the Court, but in this case the prosecution had not shown it to fall within the principle and the question certified by the Circuit Court of Appeals had described the document as of evidential value only. If such papers, then, are seized in violation of the Fourth Amendment, the Court concluded, their admission in evidence is also an infringement of the Fifth Amendment against compulsory self-incrimination.[101]

---

[101] It is interesting to note that this case, which was won on this and every other issue by the defendant, and which on another point was in a later case described by Chief Justice Taft as going to the extreme limit of the law, was argued on behalf of the defendant by the present Chief Justice of the Court, Charles Evans Hughes.

Compare *Schenck* v. *United States*, 249 U. S. 47, 63 L. ed. 470, 39 Sup. Ct. 247 (1919). Although the circulars seized in that case would clearly come within the rule laid down in the *Gouled* case as being the proper objects of a seizure, since they were intended to be used to incite insurrection in the Army, it is difficult to see upon what basis the minute-book seized at the Socialist headquarters could be taken, except merely to be used in evidence. This case, decided several years before the *Gouled* case, did not go into any real discussion of the question, but in view of the rule laid down in the latter case and the reaffirmance of the principle in the *Lefkowitz* case (cit. above), it would appear to be rather doubtful whether such evidence as the minute-book could be legally seized at the present time. It is pertinent to remark that seasonable application by the

In the recent *Lefkowitz* case [102] which has already been considered in another connection, this doctrine was further logically amplified to cover the case of search incidental to arrest. After the arrest in that case, a general exploratory search of the office by the officers produced certain documents of evidential value only. The government attempted to distinguish the decision in the *Gouled* case by arguing that although no *warrant* could be issued for the seizure of those papers, yet they could be seized in the search which may take place after a valid arrest has been made, pointing to the seizure of the ledger and bills in the *Marron* case,[103] a case that had seemed to create an exception to the evidential property rule. The Court held, however, and correctly it would seem, that the authority to search without a warrant incidental to arrest could certainly not be greater than under a search warrant issued upon adequate proof and describing the place to be searched and the things to be seized; and that since the papers of evidential value only which were seized in the instant case could not have been taken even under the safeguards of a search warrant, their seizure *a fortiori* could not be justified without any warrant at all.

But when it came to distinguishing the *Marron* case, the Court was not very successful. In that case, the Court said, the decision had held that the ledger and bills were in use to carry on the criminal enterprise, whereas here the papers were in themselves unoffending.[104] Admitting, however, that the ledger could be called part of the equipment

---

proper party for the return of the evidence does not seem to have been made in the *Schenck* case.

[102] Cit. above.

[103] Cit. above.

[104] In comparison with the reasoning of the Court in the *Gouled* case as to the types of papers seizable and the reasons therefor, it is submitted that the mere use of the records employed in carrying out the enterprise of running the saloon would be insufficient to render them seizable. In the *Lefkowitz* case, letterheads, addressed envelopes, order books, lists of names and addresses, and business cards were among the papers seized. But the Court held that even " though intended to be used to solicit orders for liquor in violation of the Act "—and certainly this would be a case where the property *was being used to carry on the criminal enterprise*—" the papers and other articles found and taken were in themselves unoffending " and evidential only, and therefore held not subject to seizure.

actually used to commit the offense, it is impossible to see how the gas and electric bills could be any more unoffending than any other papers belonging to the defendant there and how the government's "interest" in these bills, which were an essential bit of evidence to associate the defendant with the ownership of the saloon, could be established, under the principle and reasoning of the *Gouled* case, just because they were "convenient in keeping the accounts." The government clearly had no "interest" in them except as useful in evidence against the defendant, no more so than it had in the attorney's bill for services in the *Gouled* case or in the electric light bills and telephone company receipt in the *Lefkowitz* case. It may thus be said that the *Lefkowitz* case, in holding that as to matter of merely evidential value the same rule applies in searches incidental to arrest as applies in the case of search warrants,[105] modified considerably the decision in the *Marron* case.

Attention may now be directed to another type of judicial process that has involved interpretation of the Fourth Amendment, the subpoena *duces tecum,* a writ commanding a person to produce books, papers, or other documentary evidence, under pain of being held in contempt for refusal to comply. The case of *Boyd* v. *United States* [106] presented a variation of this process in the method of compulsion. The principle there laid down, however, applies equally if not more so to the subpoena *duces tecum,* namely, that to compel a person in a criminal case to furnish documents to be used against himself accomplishes the purpose of a search and seizure and violates the Fourth Amendment as to unreasonable searches and seizures and the Fifth Amendment as to compulsory self-incrimination. Where there is a statute to guarantee the defendant immunity from prosecution, however, the purpose of a search and seizure is not accomplished and there is no compulsory self-incrimination by the production of the documents, so both objections would fall to the

---

[105] Cf. the apparent exception as regards such evidence found in the search of the person, as pointed out in note 99, above. It is difficult to reconcile this exception with the general rule.

[106] 116 U. S. 616, 29 L. ed. 746, 6 Sup. Ct. 524 (1886).

ground.[107] But at the same time the subpoena must not be
unreasonable for any other reason, such as not being sufficiently particular in indicating what is wanted or being too
broad in its scope, if it is not to violate the constitutional
guaranty. In other words, the subpoena is equivalent to
a search and seizure and to be constitutional it must be a
reasonable exercise of the power.[108]

At this point it is necessary to make clear the distinction
which the Court has drawn between an individual and a
corporation. Both are entitled to protection against unreasonable search and seizure, but only the individual and not the
corporation may plead the self-incrimination clause of the
Fifth Amendment.[109] The corporation being the creature of
the state and subject to its regulation, the Court has reasoned
that the state may inquire as to whether the franchises and
charter which it has given the corporation have been properly
exercised and, in furtherance of this power, may call for
books and papers to investigate the matter.[110] Accordingly,

---

[107] *Interstate Commerce Commission* v. *Baird*, 194 U. S. 25, 48 L.
ed. 860, 24 Sup. Ct. 563 (1903) ; *Hale* v. *Henkel*, 201 U. S. 43, 50
L. ed. 652, 26 Sup. Ct. 370 (1906).

[108] *Interstate Commerce Commission* v. *Brimson*, 154 U. S. 447,
38 L. ed. 1047, 14 Sup. Ct. 1125 (1893) ; *Hale* v. *Henkel*, cit. above.

[109] *Ibid.*; *Essgee Co.* v. *United States*, 262 U. S. 151, 67 L. ed. 917,
43 Sup. Ct. 514 (1923).

[110] *Hale* v. *Henkel*, cit. above. See the concurring opinion in this
case of Justices Harlan and McKenna, and the dissenting opinion of
Chief Justice Fuller and Justice Brewer.
This dissent, besides arguing that a corporation should be entitled
to the protection of both amendments, went on to contend, and it
would seem with propriety, that even accepting this reasoning as to
the power of investigation on the part of the creator of a corporation in the case of a state corporation, this power belongs to the
state, and to the state only; and that the Federal Government
could not take advantage of the same position merely by virtue of
its powers over interstate commerce. See also *Baltimore and Ohio
Railroad Co.* v. *Interstate Commerce Commission*, 221 U. S. 612, 55 L.
ed. 878, 31 Sup. Ct. 621 (1910), and compare *Federal Trade Commission* v. *American Tobacco Co.*, 264 U. S. 298, 68 L. ed. 696, 44
Sup. Ct. 336, 32 A. L. R. 786 (1924) and *Federal Trade Commission* v. *Hammond*, 284 Fed. 886 (1922), affirmed in a memorandum
decision in 267 U. S. 586, 69 L. ed. 800, 45 Sup. Ct. 461 (1925).
This holding, however, probably from motives of expediency in corporate investigations, has never been departed from. Compare also,
Consolidated Rendering Co. v. *Vermont*, 207 U. S. 541, 52 L. ed.

a corporation does not have to be granted immunity before
its papers and records may be required, although the subpoena
must at the same time be reasonable so as not to violate the
Fourth Amendment; whereas in the case of an individual,
it must not only satisfy this essential of reasonableness, but in
order also to avoid the plea of self-incrimination, the government must first grant him *complete* immunity from prosecution.[111]

In the leading case of *Hale* v. *Henkel*,[112] the Court found
that the writ was far too sweeping in its terms to be regarded
as reasonable.   The order in that instance required, the Court
said, not one contract, or contracts with a particular corporation, or a limited number of contracts, but all contracts,
understandings, and correspondence between the corporation
and no less than six different companies, as well as all reports made and accounts rendered by such companies from the
date of the organization of the corporation, together with all
letters received from a dozen different companies.   " If the
writ had required all books, papers, and documents in the
office . . . it could scarcely be more universal in its operation
or more completely put a stop to the business of that company." [113]   Moreover, the subpoena was not only lacking in
the particularity of description necessary in both a search
warrant and a subpoena *duces tecum,* but it failed to show
evidence of materiality, which the Court held was necessary to justify the demand for the papers.   Such a general
subpoena, concluded the Court, was as indefensible as a
general warrant in similar terms.[114]

327, 28 Sup. Ct. 178 (1908) with *Hammond Packing Co.* v. *Arkansas,*
212 U. S. 322, 53 L. ed. 530, 29 Sup. Ct. 370 (1908).

An unincorporated association may also be proceeded against by
subpoena *duces tecum.* See *Brown* v. *United States,* 276 U. S. 134,
72 L. ed. 500, 48 Sup. Ct. 288 (1928).

[111] See *Nelson* v. *United States,* 201 U. S. 68, 50 L. ed. 673, 26
Sup. Ct. 391 (1906) ; *Ballman* v. *Fagin,* 200 U. S. 186, 50 L. ed.
433, 26 Sup. Ct. 151 (1905) ; *Brown* v. *Walker,* 161 U. S. 595, 40
L. ed. 820, 16 Sup. Ct. 644 (1896).

[112] Cit. above.

[113] See also *Veeder* v. *United States,* 252 Fed. 414 (1918), certiorari denied, 246 U. S. 675 (1918).

[114] In the same case, the statement was made that in view of the
power of Congress over interstate commerce, the Court did not wish

In subsequent cases, however, the Court has permitted quite a degree of latitude to the scope of such a subpoena in investigations of corporate practices. In *Consolidated Rendering Company* v. *Vermont*,[115] to the objection that the documents required were not described with sufficient particularity and the subpoena was too broad, the answer was given that although the notice was quite broad, it was limited to books and papers relating to dealings covering a period of less than three years between designated parties and with reference to a particular inquiry as to the sale of diseased meat. There was no reason why such documentary evidence should not be called for, asserted the Court, since otherwise each particular paper would have to be designated, " which presupposes an accurate knowledge of such papers, which the tribunal desiring the papers would probably rarely,. if ever, have." And in *Brown* v. *United States*,[116] a subpoena was held not unreasonable which directed a certain association to produce all correspondence with its predecessor relating to manufacture of case goods over a period of about three and a half years, with particular reference to a long and comprehensive list of general items of inquiry, to throw light on price-fixing and monopolies in violation of the Sherman Anti-Trust Act.[117]

---

to be understood as holding that an *examination of a corporation's* books, duly authorized by act of Congress, would constitute an unreasonable search and seizure. Cf. the opinion of Circuit Judge Rose in *Federal Trade Commission* v. *Hammond*, 284 Fed. 886, affirmed in 267 U. S. 586, 69 L. ed. 800, 45 Sup. Ct. 461 (mem. 1925).

[115] Cit. above.

[116] Cit. above.

[117] The Court distinguished the *Hale* case on the ground that the time embraced in that instance was the entire period of the corporation's existence and that there was no specification with regard to the subject matter, whereas here the period was reasonable and there was reasonable particularity in the statement of the inquiries to which the various documents related. See also *Hammond Packing Co.* v. *Arkansas*, cit. above; *Wilson* v. *United States*, 221 U. S. 361, 55 L. ed. 771, 31 Sup. Ct. 538 (1910) ; *Wheeler* v. *United States*, 226 U. S. 478, 57 L. ed. 309, 33 Sup. Ct. 158 (1912) ; *Grant* v. *United States*, 227 U. S. 74, 57 L. ed. 423, 33 Sup. Ct. 190 (1912).

On the question of the subpoena *duces tecum* as related to a corporation and its officers, the Court has always decided the cases in such a way as not to let the corporation hide behind its officers and vice versa, although the distinctions which the Court has been forced to draw in some instances have been very ingenious. Besides

There remains to be considered one further class of cases, which have to do with the applicability of the Fourth Amendment as a whole. Before the adoption of the Fourteenth Amendment, it was clearly recognized and uniformly held in a long line of cases, beginning with *Barron* v. *Baltimore*,[118] that the limitations of the federal Bill of Rights applied to the Federal Government only and not to the states. After the passage of that Amendment, however, with its provisions forbidding the abridgement by the states of the " privileges and immunities of citizens of the United States," the argument was strenuously advanced in a number of cases that this reenacted the first eight amendments against the states. But the Court held, in the *Slaughter House Cases*,[119] that the privileges and immunities of United States citizenship meant those possessed by the citizen by virtue of his *national* citizenship, and not those ordinary fundamental rights which the citizen of any state would have. In *Maxwell* v. *Dow*,[120] the Court further held that the Fourteenth Amendment did not necessarily comprehend those rights enumerated in the first eight amendments and, more specifically, that trial by jury was not such a privilege and immunity. Thereafter, in a number of cases the Court was presented with the specific question whether the guaranty against unreasonable search and seizure was a privilege and immunity of United States citizenship but in each case the Court seemed purposely to avoid this primary question of its jurisdiction and went out

---

the cases cited above, see also *Dreier* v. *United States*, 221 U. S. 394, 55 L. ed. 784, 31 Sup. Ct. 556 (1910) ; *American Lithographic Co.* v. *Werckmeister*, 221 U. S. 603, 55 L. ed. 873, 31 Sup. Ct. 676 (1910) ; *Essgee Co.* v. *United States*, 262 U. S. 151, 67 L. ed. 917, 43 Sup. Ct. 514 (1923).

With regard to the subpoena *duces tecum* to compel a bankrupt to produce his records, see *In re Harris*, 221 U. S. 274, 55 L. ed. 732, 31 Sup. Ct. 498 (1911) ; *Johnson* v. *United States*, 228 U. S. 457, 57 L. ed. 919, 33 Sup. Ct. 690 (1913) ; *In re Fuller*, 262 U. S. 91, 67 L. ed. 881, 43 Sup. Ct. 496 (1923).

[118] 7 Pet. 243, 8 L. ed. 672 (1833). As to the Fourth Amendment in particular, see *Smith* v. *Maryland*, 18 How. 71, 15 L. ed. 269 (1855).

[119] 16 Wall. 36, 21 L. ed. 394 (1873). Cf., however, *Colgate* v. *Harvey*, 296 U. S. 404, 80 L. ed. 225, 56 Sup. Ct. 252 (1935).

[120] 176 U. S. 581, 44 L. ed. 597, 20 Sup. Ct. 448 (1900).

of its way to decide the case on other points.[121]   However, in *National Safe Deposit Company* v. *Stead*,[122] the assertion was flatly made, without discussion, that an unreasonable search and seizure within state jurisdiction raised no federal question, since "the 4th Amendment does not apply to the states." [123]

On this principle, accordingly, it has been held that since the Fourth Amendment, as well as the Fifth, binds only the Federal Government and its agents, an illegal seizure committed by any other person does not render that evidence inadmissible in a federal prosecution of an accused person. Thus, in *Weeks* v. *United States*,[124] the evidence illegally seized by the federal marshal was thrown out, but other evidence taken by a state policeman at another time in an equally unlawful manner was admitted.   On the same principle, in the case of *Burdeau* v. *McDowell*,[125] a petition for the return of papers stolen by private detectives from the office of the defendant and later turned over to the federal authorities was held properly refused.[126]

---

[121] See *Adams* v. *New York*, cit. above; *Consolidated Rendering Co.* v. *Vermont*, cit. above.

[122] 232 U. S. 58, 58 L. ed. 504, 38 Sup. Ct. 209 (1914).   See also *People* v. *Adams*, 176 N. Y. 351, 68 N. E. 636 (1903); *Banks* v. *Alabama*, 18 Ala. App. 376, 93 So. 293 (1921), certiorari denied, 260 U. S. 736 (1922).   With regard to the self-incrimination clause of the Fifth Amendment, see *Twining* v. *New Jersey*, 211 U. S. 78, 53 L. ed. 97, 29 Sup. Ct. 14 (1908).

[123] As to whether the argument may be made, under the doctrine of certain recent cases, that an unreasonable search and seizure is an infringement of a fundamental element of that "liberty" which under the Fourteenth Amendment a state may not deny a person without due process of law, see Charles Warren, "The New 'Liberty' under the Fourteenth Amendment," *Harvard Law Review*, 1926, XXXIX, 431, in connection with which see also the language used by the Court in various cases in describing the fundamental character of the right to be secure against unreasonable searches and seizures, page 114, above.   Cf. also such cases as *Gitlow* v. *New York*, 268 U. S. 652, 69 L. ed. 1138, 45 Sup. Ct. 625 (1924); *Near* v. *Minnesota*, 283 U. S. 697, 75 L. ed. 1357, 51 Sup. Ct. 625 (1931); *Stromberg* v. *California*, 283 U. S. 359, 75 L. ed. 1117, 51 Sup. Ct. 532 (1931); *Powell* v. *Alabama*, 287 U. S. 45, 77 L. ed. 158, 53 Sup. Ct. 55 (1932); *De Jonge* v. *Oregon*, 81 L. ed. 189 (Adv. Ops., 1937).

[124] 232 U. S. 383, 58 L. ed. 652, 34 Sup. Ct. 341, L. R. A. 1915B 834, Ann. Cas. 1915C 1117 (1914).

[125] 256 U. S. 465, 65 L. ed. 1048, 41 Sup. Ct. 574 (1921).

[126] Justices Brandeis and Holmes dissented.

The possibilities of this doctrine are illustrated in a news item

Of course federal officers cannot thus directly avoid the operation of the Fourth Amendment by hiring others to do what they may not. And similarly they may themselves take such a part in the search and seizure as to make it actually a federal proceeding. In *Byars* v. *United States*,[127] a state officer procured a search warrant under a state law to search defendant's premises and then invited a federal prohibition agent along on the possibility that a violation of the Volstead Act might be discovered. The latter took an active part in the search,[128] during which were found counterfeit bottled-in-bond stamps. Upon the basis of the finding of these stamps a federal prosecution was later instituted, since this counterfeiting constituted no offense against the state law. The Court held that while mere participation of a federal officer in a state search would not make it a federal undertaking, yet where the latter is invited to assist not in the capacity of a *private* person but is purposely asked to participate upon the chance that an offense against the federal law might be found, it is a *joint* undertaking; and in a federal prosecution, it is a federal search and seizure to be tested by federal and not by state law. Since the warrant in this case was bad because it did not show probable cause, the evidence, the Court held, should have been returned upon seasonable application.

In *Gambino* v. *United States*,[129] the operation of the doctrine was still further limited and the law more clearly outlined. In that case the illegal search of an automobile without probable cause and the seizure of liquor was effected entirely

which appeared in the Baltimore *Evening Sun*, February 13, 1933, reporting the formation of a prohibition organization known as the "New Vigilantes of America" to aid in the enforcement of the Volstead Act by reporting offenses which were discovered. Cf. the *Gambino* case, which will be discussed presently. See also Forrest Revere Black, "Burdeau v. McDowell: A Judicial Milepost on the Road to Absolutism," *Boston University Law Review*, 1932, XII, 32.

[127] 273 U. S. 28, 71 L. ed. 520, 47 Sup. Ct. 248 (1927).

[128] In *Gambino* v. *United States*, 275 U. S. 310, 72 L. ed. 293, 48 Sup. Ct. 137, 52 A. L. R. 1381 (1927), Mr. Justice Brandeis would appear to be in error when he states that in the *Byars* case the search was without warrant and that it was conducted merely in the presence of the federal officer.

[129] Cit. above.

by New York state troopers without the cooperation of any federal officer. The defendants were then immediately turned over to the federal authorities for prosecution. In deciding the case, the Court pointed out that the state prohibition law had been repealed and that the state policemen were under orders from the governor to enforce the law just as before and turn over the offenders to the Federal Government. The troopers, consequently, had here searched and arrested *solely* in order to hold the defendants for a violation of federal law and in behalf of the United States, and the prosecution by the latter which followed was a ratification of their action. In such a case, the Court held, the officers were bound by the safeguards of the Federal Constitution and its Fourth and Fifth Amendments.[130]

So stands the development of the Fourth Amendment today in the decisions of the final authority on constitutional interpretation in this country, a development which has been marked in general, and especially of late, by a fine sensibility for the spirit and purpose of this fundamental safeguard in order to give it that effectiveness which its history and terms require.

---

[130] The opinion of the Court, written by Mr. Justice Brandeis, shows clearly the basis of the decision in distinguishing the following cases. In *Center* v. *United States*, 267 U. S. 575, 69 L. ed. 795, 45 Sup. Ct. 230 (1925), a memorandum decision *per curiam*, the liquor was taken for prosecution in the state courts and it was four months before it was turned over to the federal authorities. In the *Weeks* case, cit. above, the seizure did not appear to be made solely to aid a federal prosecution; the state law also made the offense criminal, and the seizure may have been in enforcement of that law. And in *Burdeau* v. *McDowell*, cit. above, the seizure was made by private detectives and no federal official had had anything to do with it or had even heard of it until several months thereafter.

TABLE OF CASES

PAGE

Adams v. *New York*, 192 U. S. 585 . . . . 110-111, 112, 127, 141
Agnello v. *United States*, 269 U. S. 20 . . . . 112, 113, 124, 126, 127
Albrecht v. *United States*, 273 U. S. 1 . . . . 117, 131
American Lithographic Co. v. *Werckmeister*, 221 U. S. 603 . .   140
American Tobacco Co. v. *Werckmeister*, 207 U. S. 284   107
Amos v. *United States*, 255 U. S. 313 . . . . 113, 117
Ballman v. *Fagin*, 200 U. S. 186   138
Baltimore and Ohio R. R. Co. v. *Interstate Commerce Commission*, 221 U. S. 612   137
Banks v. *Alabama*, 18 Ala. App. 376   141
Barron v. *Baltimore*, 7 Pet. 243   140
Blackmer v. *United States*, 284 U. S. 421   107
Bollman and Swartwout, Ex parte, 4 Cr. 75 . . . . 106, 131
Bonham's (Dr.) Case, 8 Coke 107   59
Boyd v. *United States*, 116 U. S. 616 . . : . . . .
47, 107-110, 114, 115, 119, 133, 136
Brook's (Lord) Case, 2 Parl. Hist. 667   33
Brown's Case, P. 23, Car. B. R.   37
Brown v. *United States*, 276 U. S. 134 . . . . 138, 139
Brown v. *Walker*, 161 U. S. 595   138
Burdeau v. *McDowell*, 256 U. S. 465 . . . . 141, 142, 143
Burford, Ex parte, 3 Cr. 448 . . . . 106, 129
Byars v. *United States*, 273 U. S. 28 . . . . 130, 142
Carr's Case, 7 State Trials 1127   38
Carroll v. *United States*, 267 U. S. 132 . . . . 125, 126, 130, 131
Center v. *United States*, 267 U. S. 575   143
Chapman, Re, 166 U. S. 661   119
Cogen v. *United States*, 278 U. S. 221   116
Colgate v. *Harvey*, 296 U. S. 404   140
Consolidated Rendering Co. v. *Vermont*, 207 U. S. 541 . . . . . .
117, 137, 139, 141
Cooper v. *Boot*, 4 Doug. 347 . . . . 28-29, 37
Darnell's Case, 3 State Trials 1   30
De Jonge v. *Oregon*, 81 L. ed. 189 (Adv. Ops., 1937)   141
Dreier v. *United States*, 221 U. S. 394   140
Dumbra v. *United States*, 268 U. S. 435 . . . . 121, 131
Elliot's Case, 3 State Trials 235   31
Entick v. *Carrington*, 19 State Trials 1029 . . . . 26, 38, 47-48, 109
Essgee Co. v. *United States*, 262 U. S. 151 . . . . 137, 140
Ewing v. *Cradock*, Quincy 552   64
Federal Trade Commission v. *American Tobacco Co.*, 264 U. S.
298 . . . . 110, 137
Federal Trade Commission v. *Hammond*, 284 Fed. 886 . . . . . . 137, 139
Flint v. *Stone Tracy Co.*, 220 U. S. 107   120
Fong Yue Ting v. *United States*, 149 U. S. 698 . . . . 107, 116-117
Frisbie v. *Butler*, Kirby 213   82
Fuller, In re, 262 U. S. 91   140

145

PAGE

Gambino v. *United States*, 275 U. S. 310 . . . . 114, 131, 142
Gitlow v. *New York*, 268 U. S. 652 141
Go-Bart Importing Co. v. *United States*, 282 U. S. 344 . . . . . .
 . . . . 110, 114, 116, 120, 121, 124, 128, 129, 133
Gouled v. *United States*, 255 U. S. 298 . . . .
 . . . . 110, 111-112, 115, 118, 121, 129, 133-134, 135, 136
Grant v. *United States*, 227 U. S. 74 139
Grau v. *United States*, 287 U. S. 124 . . . . 110, 124, 129, 130, 131
Hale v. *Henkel*, 201 U. S. 43 . . . . 117, 119, 137, 138, 139
Hammond Packing Co. v. *Arkansas*, 212 U. S. 322 . . . . 138, 139
Harris, In re, 221 U. S. 274 140
Harris' Case, 7 State Trials 929 38
Hester v. *United States*, 265 U. S. 57 . . . . 119, 125
Huckle v. *Money*, 2 Wils. 205 . . . . 21, 44
Husty v. *United States*, 282 U. S. 694 . . . . 125, 126, 130, 131
Interstate Commerce Commission v. *Baird*, 194 U. S. 25 137
Interstate Commerce Commission v. *Brimson*, 154 U. S. 447 137
Jackson, In re, 96 U. S. 727 . . . . 107, 119
Johnson v. *United States*, 228 U. S. 457 140
Kimbolton's (Lord) Case, 4 Somers' Tracts 342 33
Lefkowitz v. *United States*, 52 Fed. (2d) 52 133
Luther v. *Borden*, 7 How. 1 . . . . 78, 106
Maguire v. *United States*, 273 U. S. 95 123
Marron v. *United States*, 275 U. S. 192 . . . . 127-129, 135-136
Massachusetts Bay v. *Paxton*, Quincy 548 63
Maul v. *United States*, 274 U. S. 501 125
Maxwell v. *Dow*, 176 U. S. 581 140
McDaniel v. *United States*, 294 Fed. 769 . . . . · 114
McGrain v. *Daugherty*, 273 U. S. 135 131
Milligan, Ex parte, 4 Wall. 2 . . . . 78, 106
Money v. *Leach*, 3 Burr. 1692 . . . . 21, 45-47
Murray v. *Hoboken Land Co.*, 18 How. 272 107
Nathanson v. *United States*, 290 U. S. 41 130
National Safe Deposit Co. v. *Stead*, 232 U. S. 58 141
Near v. *Minnesota*, 283 U. S. 697 141
Nelson v. *United States*, 201 U. S. 68 138
Ocampo v. *United States*, 234 U. S. 91 130
Olmstead v. *United States*, 277 U. S. 438 . . . . 118, 119
Paxton's Case, Quincy 51 . . . . 21, 23, 57 ff.
People v. *Adams*, 176 N. Y. 351 141
People v. *Defore*, 242 N. Y. 13 . . . . 114, 122
Perlman v. *United States*, 247 U. S. 7 119
Powell v. *Alabama*, 287 U. S. 45 141
Remus v. *United States*, 291 Fed. 50 . . . . 112, 117
Rex v. *Earbury*, 2 Barn. K. B. 396 42
Roger v. *William*, Select Pleas, I, 142 19
Sanborn v. *Carlton*, 15 Gray 399 60
Schenck v. *United States*, 249 U. S. 47 . . . . 106, 121, 134
Segurola v. *United States*, 275 U. S. 106 114
Selden's Case, 3 State Trials 235 31
Semaine's Case, 5 Coke 91 35
Sgro v. *United States*, 287 U. S. 206 . . . . 122, 130
Silverthorne Lumber Co. v. *United States*, 251 U. S. 385 . . . .
 . . . . 115-116, 124, 127

PAGE

Slaughter House Cases, 16 Wall. 36...................... 140

Smith v. *Maryland*, 18 How. 71...........................106, 140

Steele v. *United States*, 267 U. S. 498, 505........121, 124, 131, 132

Strafford's (Earl of) Case, 3 State Trials 1391............ 33

Stromberg v. *California*, 283 U. S. 359.................. 141

Stroud v. *United States*, 251 U. S. 15...................... 107

Swallow's (Justice) Case, P. 24, Car. I.................... 35

Taylor v. *United States*, 286 U. S. 1.....................124, 126

Twining v. *New Jersey*, 211 U. S. 78..................... 141

United States v. *Bollman*, Fed. Cas. 14,622................ 106

United States v. *Innelli*, 286 Fed. 731..................... 50

United States v. *Lee*, 274 U. S. 640...................... 125

United States v. *Lefkowitz*, 285 U. S. 452..................
110, 114, 127-129, 133, 134, 135, 136

United States v. *Mills*, 185 Fed. 318...................... 112

United States ex rel. Bilokumsky v. *Tod*, 263 U. S. 149......116, 119

Veeder v. *United States*, 252 Fed. 414.................121, 130, 138

Warwick's (Earl of) Case, 2 Parl. Hist. 667................ 33

Weeks v. *United States*, 232 U. S. 383....................
111-112, 116, 127, 132, 141, 143

West v. *Cabell*, 153 U. S. 78............................ 132

Wheeler v. *United States*, 226 U. S. 478....................117, 139

Wilkes v. *Wood*, Lofft 1................................. 45

Wilson v. *United States*, 221 U. S. 361....................117, 139

Wire-Tapping Case, see *Olmstead* v. *United States*.

Wise v. *Mills*, 185 Fed. 318.............................112, 127

Writs of Assistance Case, see *Paxton's Case*.

TABLE OF STATUTES

I. ENGLISH

(Chronologically arranged)

PAGE

Laws of King Edmund (Ancient Laws and Institutes of England, I, 251) 19

Laws of King Cnut (Ancient Laws and Institutes of England, I, 409) 19

9 Edw. III, St. II, ch. 11 23

27 Edw. III, St. I, ch. 3 23

34 Edw. III, ch. 1 22

4 Hen. IV, ch. 21 23

11 Hen. VII, ch. 27 24

3 Hen. VIII, ch. 12 22

3 Hen. VIII, ch. 14 24

39 Eliz., ch. 13 24

1 Jac. I, ch. 19 28

3 Jac. I, ch. 4 28

3 & 4 Jac. I, ch. 5 28

7 Jac. I, ch. 4 28

16 Char. I, ch. 10 32

16 Char. I, ch. 11 32

Ordinance of 1643 (Acts and Ordinances of the Interregnum, I, 185) 33

Ordinance of 1647 (Acts and Ordinances of the Interregnum, I, 1022) 33

Act of 1649 (Acts and Ordinances of the Interregnum, II, 247, 251) 33

Act of 1652-53 (Acts and Ordinances of the Interregnum, II, 698) 33

12 Char. II, ch. 4 37

12 Char. II, ch. 19 .... 37, 40

12 Char. II, ch. 22 37

12 Char. II, ch. 23 37

13 & 14 Char. II, ch. 10 38

13 & 14 Char. II, ch. 11 .... 37, 53

13 & 14 Char. II, ch. 33 37

15 Char. II, ch. 11 .... 23, 40

25 Char. II, ch. 7 56

1 Wm. & M., ch. 10 39

1 Wm. & M., ch. 24 40

3 & 4 Wm. & M., ch. 10 40

4 & 5 Wm. & M., ch. 23 40

7 & 8 Wm. III, ch. 22 .... 53 ff., 64 ff.

5 Geo. I, ch. 28 40

10 Geo. I, ch. 10 40

7 Geo. III, ch. 46 .... 69 ff.

149

II. COLONIAL

PAGE

1 Hening 257 (Va.)...................................... 33
Prov. Stat. 11 Wm. III (Mass. Bay)...................... 58
3 Acts and Resolves of Mass. Bay, 406, 471, 522, 581, 622, 701,
    762, 845, 1008.................................... 56
Prov. Stat. 32 Geo. II, ch. 1 (Mass. Bay)................. 56

III. UNITED STATES

1 Stat. L. 145, 170, 305, 315, 627, 677, 678................ 125
41 Stat. L. 305... 124
18 U. S. C. A. secs. 611-631............................121-123

See also Index, under popular names of statutes.

INDEX

Achan, 13.
Adams, John, 46 n., 51 n., 58 ff., 66, 80.
Adams, Samuel, 46 n., 80, 96 n.
Alfred the Great, 19.
Alien and Sedition Laws, 92 n.
Aliens, 116.
Allen, Chief Justice, 74.
Anglo-Norman period, 22.
Anglo-Saxon law, 18-19.
Anson, Justice, 47.
Anti-Trust Act, 106, 138-139.
Areopagetica, Milton's, 33.
Auchmuty, Robert, 63 n.
Aufidius, 15 n.

Benson, Egbert, 101-103.
Bernard, Governor, 51 n., 52 n., 56 ff., 63 n., 68 ff.
Bill of Rights (federal), argument for in Constitutional Convention of 1787, 83 ff.; attempt by Lee in Congress to insert in Constitution, 87-88; debates on omission of, 88 ff.; passage and adoption of, 98 ff.; effect of passage, 103 ff. For state bills of rights, see under respective states.
Blackstone, 41 n.
Bollan, William, 63, 67.
Boston merchants, opposition to writs of assistance, 57 ff.
Bradley, Mr. Justice, 108 ff.
Brandeis, Mr. Justice, 118, 141 n., 142 n., 143 n.
Brook, Lord, 33 n.

Cardozo, Mr. Justice, 122 n.
Charles I, 29 ff.
Chesterfield, 40 n.
Cicero, 15, 16, 17.
Clarke, Mr. Justice, 112-113, 133-134.
Coke, Sir Edward, 21, 31 ff., 37 n., 59.
Collateral issue rule, 110 ff., 122 n.
Colonial policy of England, 51 ff., 67.

Common law, 34 ff.
Confederation, Articles of, 83.
Connecticut, writs of assistance in, 73; Constitution of 1776, 82 n.
Constitution (U. S.), omission of bill of rights, 83 ff.; submission of Constitution to Congress, 87-88; submission to states, 88 ff.
Constitutional Convention of 1787, 83 ff.
Continental Congress, petition to king, 75; action in the case of the Virginia Exiles, 76 ff.
Coriolanus, 15 n.
Corporations, 116-117, 137 ff.

Dane, Nathan, 87.
Day, Mr. Justice, 111.
Declaration of Independence, 80.
De Grey, William, 47 n., 64 ff., 69 ff.
Delegated powers theory, 85, 90 ff., 99 ff.
Dickinson, John, 70 n.
Drayton, Judge William Henry, 15 n., 75.
Dyers, Company of, 23.

Elizabethan period, 24 ff.
Elliot, Sir John, 31.
Entick, John, 47 ff.
Excise tax, 34, 40 ff.

Federalist, 88 n.
Fifth Amendment, 108 ff., 117, 137 ff., 141 ff. See also under Fourth Amendment.
Fourteenth Amendment, 140 ff.
Fourth Amendment, historical background, chaps. i, ii; state constitutional precedents for, 79 ff.; passage by Congress, 101 ff.; development of (by Supreme Court), chap. iv: early cases, 106 ff.; martial law, 106 n.; under emergency conditions, 106 n.; relation to criminal and civil proceedings,

107, 116 n.; opening of mail, 107, 119; application to state process, 106 n.; relation of Fourth Amendment to self-incrimination provision of Fifth Amendment, 108 ff., 111 ff., 134 ff.; elements of a search and seizure, 108, 110 n., 118-120, 136-139; compulsory production of documentary evidence, 108 ff.; property seizable, 108-109, 121, 124, 133 ff.; liberal construction of Amendment, 109-110; collateral issue rule, 110 ff.; petition for return of property unconstitutionally seized, 111 ff.; importance of guaranty against unreasonable search, 114-115; photographing of evidence unconstitutionally seized, 115-116; appeal to higher court, 116; who may claim protection of Amendment, 116-117; deportation proceedings, 116 n.; waiver of privileges under Amendment, 117 n.; wire-tapping, 118; interrogation, abandoned property, and voluntary production, 119-120; reasonableness, 120 ff.; statutory requirements, 120-123; federal warrants, by and to whom issuable, 120-121; examination by magistrates and issuance of warrant, 121; execution of warrant, 121-123; penalties for abuse of process, 123; warrants, when necessary, 123-126; dwellings, offices, garages, fields, 123-124; search incidental to arrest, 124, 126-129, 133, 135-136; movable vehicles, 125-126, 129-130; oath or affirmation, 131-132; evidential property rule, 133 ff.; applicability of Amendment to state or private action, 140 ff. See also, probable cause, particularity of description, subpoena *duces tecum*, corporations, privileges and immunities, etc.

Fuller, Chief Justice, 137 n.

General commissions of inquiry, 22.

General warrants, 16, 24 ff., 29 ff., 33, 35 ff., 43 ff., 76 ff.; in bills of rights, 79 ff., 120. See also, writs of assistance, *lettres de cachet*.

Georgia, writs of assistance in, 75-76.

Gerry, Elbridge, 84-85, 88-89, 98 n., 101, 103.

Gladstone, 83.

Gorham, Mr., in Constitutional Convention, 83-84.

Gray, Horace, 55 n.

Grayson, Mr., in Virginia Convention, 91 n.

Gridley, Jeremiah, 53 n., 58 ff.

Hale, Sir Matthew, 32 n., 35 ff.

Halifax, Lord, 43 ff.

Hammurabi, Code of, housebreaking under, 14 n.

Hamsocn, 18-19.

Hancock, John, 46 n., 72.

Hardwicke, Lord, 42.

Harlan, Mr. Justice, 137 n.

Hearth money, 37, 39.

Hebrew law, 14.

Henry, Patrick, 80, 91 n., 92 ff., 102 n.

High Commission, Court of, 25 ff., 32.

Holmes, Mr. Justice, 106 n., 115-116, 141.

House of Commons, resolutions regarding general warrants, 48 ff.

Hughes, Chief Justice, 122 n., 134 n.

Hutchinson, Chief Justice, 51 n., 57 ff., 66 n., 68 ff.

Interregnum, 32 ff.

Interstate Commerce Act, 106.

Jefferson, Thomas, 78 n., 79 n., 80, 89, 90 n., 98 n.

John (King), 20.

Johnson, Dr. Samuel, 40 n., 46.

Joshua, 13, 14.

Kidd, Thomas, 27 n.

Kimbolton, Lord, 33 n.

Lance et licio, procedure of, 17-18.

Lansing, John, 89 n.

Laud, Archbishop, 34 n.
Leach, Dryden, 44 ff.
Lee, Richard Henry, 87 ff.
Lettres de cachet, 29, 50 n.
Licensing Act, 37 ff., 41 ff., 48.
Livermore, Mr., in debate in Congress on Fourth Amendment, 101 n.
Long Parliament, 32 ff.
Lot, 14.

MacClay, William, 102 n.
Madison, James, 21 n., 78, 79-80, 84, 87, 90 n., 96 n.; sponsors amendments in Congress, 97 ff.
Magna Carta, 19-21, 23 n., 30.
Malcom, Daniel, 65, 68 ff.
Mansfield, (Lord), 21, 46.
Marlowe, Christopher, 27.
Marshall, John, 96 n.
Martin, Luther, 84 n., 89.
Martin Marprelate libels, 27 n.
Maryland, writs of assistance in, 55 n., 74; Declaration of Rights, 81; ratification of Constitution, 96 n.
Mason, George, 79 ff., 84, 88, 92 ff.
Massachusetts, Declaration of Rights, 30 n., 82; ratification of Constitution, 96 n.
Massachusetts Bay, Body of Liberties, 30 n.; writs of assistance in, 51-73; action of legislature on writs of assistance, 56, 66; reduction of judges' salaries by legislature, 67.
McKean, Chief Justice, 77.
McKenna, Mr. Justice, 137 n.
Mein, Patrick, 55 n.
Miller, Mr. Justice, 109 n.
Milton, John, 33.
Molasses Act, 51 ff.
Monitor or British Freeholder, 47.

New Hampshire, writs of assistance in, 74; Bill of Rights, 82; ratification of Constitution, 96 n.
New Jersey, writs of assistance in, 74; no bill of rights in first constitution, 80 n.
New York, writs of assistance in, 74; Convention on ratifica-
tion of Constitution, 89 n., 95 n., 96 n.
Nicholas, George, 86 n., 92 n.
North Briton, 43 ff., 54.
North Carolina, Declaration of Rights, 81-82; early failure to ratify Constitution, 96 n., 98; effect of passage of federal Bill of Rights on ratification, 103-104.

Otis, James (Jr.), 21, 23 n., 37 n., 46 n., 51 n., 52 n., 53 n., 57 ff., 66 ff., 71-72.
Otis, James (Sr.), 57.

Particularity of description in warrants, 17, 35 ff., 38, 120, 121, 127, 132-133, 138-139.
Paxton, Charles, 56, 63.
Pennsylvania, writs of assistance in, 74; Bill of Rights, 80-81; ratification of Constitution, 89 ff.
Petition of Right, 30.
Pinckney, Mr., in Constitutional Convention, 85.
Pitney, Mr. Justice, 116 n.
Pitt, William, 41, 48 ff., 52 n., 57.
Prat, Benjamin, 58 n.
Pratt, Chief Justice (Lord Camden), 21, 26 n., 38 n., 44 ff., 62, 63, 109.
Printing, regulation of, 24, 28, 32 ff., 37 ff. See Licensing Act.
Privileges and immunities of United States citizenship, 111 n., 140 ff.
Privy Council, 25 ff., 30 ff., 39 n.
Probable cause, 36, 120 ff., 129 ff.
Prohibition Act, 124 n.
Prynne, 34 n.

Queen's Printer, 24 n.
Quincy, Josiah, 46 n., 59 n.

Rachab, 14.
Randolph, Edmund, 80, 89 n., 93-95.
Restoration, 37 ff.
Reynolds, Sir Joshua, 46.
Rhode Island, writs of assistance in, 74; early failure to ratify Constitution, 96 n., 98; effect of passage of federal Bill of

Rights, 95 n., 102-103.
Roman law, 15-18; early con-
cepts, 15; criminal procedure,
15 ff.; modern safeguards,
15 n.; general search powers,
16 ff.; search for documentary
evidence, 17; search for stolen
goods, 17-18.
Ruggles, Chief Justice, 66 n.
Rum distilling in the Colonies,
51 ff.

Scroggs, Chief Justice, 38, 48.
Search powers, delegation of,
23 n., 60 n.
Sedgwick, Theodore, 101 n.
Selden, John, 31.
Self-incrimination, 23 n. See Fifth
Amendment.
Seven Years War, 52.
Sewell, Chief Justice, 56-57.
Sherman, Roger, 73 n., 84 ff.,
101 n.
Shirley, Governor, 55 ff.
Sidney, Algernon, 39 ff.
Sixth Amendment, 29 n., 50 n.
Smilie, Mr., in Pennsylvania Con-
vention, 90 n., 91.
Smith, Adam, 40 n., 52 n.
Smith, Melanchthon, 87.
Smuggling in the Colonies, 52 ff.
Sodom, 14.
South Carolina, writs of assist-
ance in, 75; ratification of Con-
stitution, 96 n.
Stamp Act Congress, 52 n.
Stamp Act Riot, 68.
Star Chamber, Court of, 24 ff.,
32, 48.
Stationers' Company, 25.
Stokes, Chief Justice, 75-76.
Stone, Mr. Justice, 122 n.
Strafford, Earl of, 33.
Subpoena *duces tecum*, seizure
of documentary evidence under,
115, 119, 136-139.

Sugar Act of 1764, 67.

Taft, Chief Justice, 118, 134 n.
Talmud, 14
Taney, Chief Justice, 106 n.
Thatcher, Oxenbridge, 58, 61 ff.,
69.
Tonnage and poundage, 30, 31.
Townshend Acts, 70 ff.
Trumbull, Chief Justice, 73 ff.

Vermont, search and seizure provision in Constitution of, 82.
Verres, prosecution of, 16.
Virginia, writs of assistance in,
74-75; Bill of Rights, 79 ff.,
92-93, 96; Convention on ratification of Constitution, 92 ff.,
99.
Virginia Exiles, 76 ff.

Waite, Chief Justice, 109 n.
Walpole, 40 ff.
Warwick, Earl of, 33 n.
Washington, George, 77 n., 85 n.,
86 n., 91 n., 97.
White, Chief Justice, 116 n.
Whitehill, Mr., in Pennsylvania
Convention, 91.
Whitgift, Archbishop, 27.
Wilkes, John, 43 ff.
William (King), 39.
Williamson, Mr., in Constitu-
tional Convention, 83.
Wilmot, Justice, 47.
Wilson, James, 86, 90 ff.
Wilson-Roosevelt doctrine, 90 n.
Wolkins, George G., 61 n.
Woodbury, Mr. Justice, 106 n.
Writs of assistance, 28-29, 37,
51 ff., 89 n. See also under each
colony.
Wythe, George, 94, 95.

Yates, Justice, 47.
Yates, Robert, 89.